AVEC ERIC

AVEC ERIC

ERIC RIPERT

with Angie Mosier and Soa Davies
photography by Angie Mosier

designed and produced by Anomaly

WILEY

John Wiley & Sons, Inc.

Published by John Wiley & Sons, Inc., Hoboken, New Jersey
Published simultaneously in Canada

This book is printed on acid-free paper. ♾

For general information on our other products and services or for technical support, please contact our Customer Care Department within the United States at (800) 762-2974, outside the United States at (317) 572-3993 or fax (317) 572-4002.

Wiley also publishes its books in a variety of electronic formats. Some content that appears in print may not be available in electronic books. For more information about Wiley products, visit our web site at www.wiley.com.

Library of Congress Cataloging-in-Publication Data

Ripert, Eric.
Avec Eric / Eric Ripert.
    p. cm.
Includes bibliographical references and index.
ISBN 978-0-470-88935-0 (cloth)
1. Ripert, Eric. 2. Le Bernardin (Restaurant) 3. Cookery. 4. Cookbooks.
I. Avec Eric (Television program) II. Title.
TX652.R566 2010
641.5–dc22   2010025728

Manufactured in China.

10 9 8 7 6 5 4 3 2 1

To everyone I have met in my lucky life
who makes the world better. —E.R.

CONTENTS

FOREWORD

by Anthony Bourdain

HE'S ONE OF THE WORLD'S BEST CHEFS.

He's had four stars from *The New York Times* longer than anyone in history. Three stars from Michelin. The public loves his food. And they love him. Time goes on, the years pass, but Le Bernardin stays, always, exciting and relevant. He's a popular judge on *Top Chef,* a fundraiser, philanthropist and activist for various good causes, a practicing Buddhist with an unholy love for high-end tequilas. A *Chevalier de la Legion d'Honneur* of France—as if that other stuff were not somehow enough for one life—and of course, he's got a TV show of his own now.

Remarkably, the TV show, *Avec Eric,* for which this volume is a companion, does NOT suck! This, of Eric Ripert's many achievements, is perhaps, the most extraordinary. Ordinarily, once TV has you in its suffocating grip, you succumb. The eyes glaze over, the soul soon becomes resigned to a long trudge downhill towards mediocrity—and death.

Yet, Eric, as with everything else in his life, continues to do things his way, the way he wants, making few—if any—concessions to the conventional wisdom, and always—always—doing it with style. You can tell that from the first few seconds of the title sequence—that this show will be... different.

I enjoy making fun of Eric's hair, as it always seems to be perfect. Not to be cruel (okay, maybe a little), but it's a perfect metaphor for Eric's unflappability. You throw that bastard down a hole, into a busy kitchen, a mosh pit, a swimming pool, or the grill station at my old restaurant (all of which I've done), and he will emerge unscathed, seemingly unperturbed; immaculate (see wild boar incident later).

Maybe he's right about this "karma" thing, after all. Because what everyone who knows Eric Ripert will tell you—friends, employees, customers and acquaintances alike—is that he's basically a good and very decent guy (a very rare and very difficult thing to be at any level of the restaurant business). He's good to the people around him—and I guess maybe that's coming back to him. Only explanation I can think of. Because it defies logic.

Otherwise: how can he go on doing what he's doing? He makes the food he wants, the way he wants. His books vary from the gorgeous, brilliantly uncompromising and self-indulgent *Return to Cooking* (where you can really get an idea of what the inside of Eric's skull looks like) to the groundbreaking *On the Line*, where he explains and illustrates exactly how he runs his kitchen at Le Bernardin: all the nuts and bolts, and as significantly, *who* runs the kitchen with him. His eagerness to share the credit—specifically to point out who does what, and how, acknowledging every part of a large, ever grinding, complicated but (always) smoothly running machine—is unprecedented. And risky. The generally accepted wisdom is that the great chef should, whenever possible, maintain the illusion that he does everything himself.

And now—now I gather, Eric's running around the world, doing whatever he wants, eating and drinking with his friends and making television and writing books about his experiences. He calls this "finding inspiration" or some such. I call it a damn good life. I've been lucky enough to do pretty much the same kind of traveling for the last few years, but unlike Eric, I don't have to return to New York and *cook* or recreate recipes or demonstrate what I've learned— much less remember anything from my voyage other than that my head hurts. So, add "educator" to his other accomplishments; you actually learn stuff watching *Avec Eric*—as you will, no doubt, reading this book.

And just as when you spend time in his company, he makes it easy—and fun. Whether as instructional material, inspiration, straight up food porn, or simply a good time, *Avec Eric* gives you a sense of what it's like to travel in the strangely enchanted world of Eric Ripert.

There's a moment on the show—a personal favorite: Eric is out hunting for wild boar, when one of the big, wooly, menacingly tusked monsters suddenly charges him. Believe me, you do NOT want one of these guys to get their hooks into your soft parts; I've seen what they can do and it ain't pretty. But I wasn't for a second concerned. I knew the boar would never touch him. It's like that with him. I believe in the end, he convinced the boar to leave his life of violence—and make a donation to City Harvest.

I'm personally grateful to Eric for many reasons. He and his wife introduced me to my wife, making everything that came after (the birth of my daughter most notably) possible. He is and has been since the beginning, a good friend to me— something that cannot have been easy at times—and has surely come with a price. I can afford to anger people, having no reputation to lose. Not so with him. I have put him—many times I'm sure—in difficult circumstances diplomatically.

But I'm also grateful to him for what he's done professionally; kept fine dining fun and exciting and dynamic—and inspiring—even to a jaded burn-out like me. Good food is a continuum—from the very complicated to the very simple, something I think you'll see demonstrated again and again in this book.

—Anthony Bourdain

INTRODUCTION

COOKING IS HOW I EXPRESS MYSELF CREATIVELY. I BEGAN TO LEARN TO COOK AS A CHILD ALONGSIDE MY MOTHER AND GRANDMOTHER, THEN MOVED ON TO WORK IN PROFESSIONAL KITCHENS WHEN I WAS 17 YEARS OLD. Le Bernardin, our restaurant in New York City, is where I express myself as a classically trained, professional chef; but really, the training never stops. Together, our restaurant team continues to learn from one another through the process of developing recipes and by sharing our collective experiences and ideas. My training also continues elsewhere—through exposure to new people and places. A few times a year I take some time to travel to locations both exotic and familiar so that I can experience the people, the cultures and—of course—the food. These influences have a profound impact on me personally. By submerging myself in the culture of a place, I gain new insights about the world and also find inspiration for new recipes. I want to share how these adventures spark my creative process, and hopefully inspire you to be expressive and adventurous in your own cooking.

Just as winemakers speak of terroir contributing to the flavor and quality of wine, I believe that food—not only the actual product, but also the various preparations and cultural history of the recipes—draws from all the aspects of a particular place. Cooking is a holistic process of planning, preparing, dining and sharing food. I place food at the center of our humanity, as it nourishes not only our physical bodies but also our emotional and spiritual lives. Food is truly a cultural phenomenon that informs our traditions and our relationship with the earth. I genuinely believe that food connects us all.

My journeys are a search for meaningful food experiences, but this doesn't necessarily mean that these experiences are fancy or extreme. It means that they engage the five senses, tap into our collective culture, transcend geographic boundaries, as well as offer the chance to commune with others and gain inspiration. The focus of the journey is always about enjoying, celebrating and respecting the world.

In New York City, where I live, it is easy to become disconnected from our food sources. We have some of the best culinary products available to us as they are brought in from all over the world, but you really have to get out of the city and visit the source to appreciate what it takes to cultivate and produce the food that ends up in our local markets. In order to get the full flavor of a particular ingredient, you have to walk the fields, talk to the farmer, see the animals and taste everything in its purest form. I use these travel opportunities to gain inspiration from different people, places and cultures, which directly informs my cooking at the restaurant and at home. This is the source of my creativity as a chef—the source of my inspiration.

Everyone is invited to share the results of my experiences in one of our restaurants; however, the focus of this book is to translate those adventures into simple recipes that cooks at every skill level can prepare and share with friends and family. Each chapter of this book reflects a distinct journey that inspires a set of recipes. They are in no particular order and are meant to be self-contained so that you can jump in wherever you want. I begin by sharing some of my travel experiences to provide a glimpse into the place, the people and the food that set the inspiration into motion. Then, I provide a "menu" of sorts in the form of a selection of recipes that relate to that journey. Along the way, I've written notes about a particular ingredient, a place or cooking method to give you a little more information. You can always get more recipes, wine pairings and watch videos of these adventures at www.aveceric.com.

My hope is that by joining me in these adventures, you too will be transported and inspired to be creative with your own cooking, but also to incorporate your own experiences into your kitchen.

Santé, Cook from life!

Chapter 1

BIG FLAVOR

Greve, Chianti, Italy

VINCENT ROBINSON,
Le Bernardin's SAUCIER.

CUISINE IS, AT ITS HEART, ABOUT FLAVOR. THE ACT OF RECOGNIZING THE ATTRIBUTES OF A SPECIFIC INGREDIENT AND UNDERSTANDING THE WAY IT WILL BLEND OR CONTRAST WITH OTHER INGREDIENTS IS WHAT COOKING IS ALL ABOUT. Developing flavors—the art of manipulating and orchestrating components to create something complete and delicious—is a life's work. At Le Bernardin in New York, there is an entire team of chefs who have made this art their life's work. One of those chefs is the saucier, Vincent Robinson, who has worked at Le Bernardin for 23 years. Vinny, as we call him in the kitchen, started out making soups and stocks for the restaurant, but we acknowledged that he had a real gift for combining complex flavors in a thoughtful way and, for several years now, he has been in charge of making all the sauces at Le Bernardin. The task is a great challenge and Vinny must know everything about the dish as a whole to make sure the sauce paired with it is harmonious.

What Vincent executes in the kitchen is very much like when a great musician—schooled in all the technicalities of music theory and performance—actually takes the stage to play with others. All the lessons and rehearsals are required to get to the stage, but what happens on that stage is about instinct, spirit and listening to what is happening at that very moment. Cooking great food is exactly the same, and each gig is different. The technical part of making the sauce is necessary, but Vincent also has the gift of instinct and passion in his cooking. It is all of these things together that create "big flavor."

In addition to technique and instinct, the ingredients themselves must be regarded. I have always been curious about regional flavors and how a culture traditionally uses what is available. The Tuscan region of Italy is known for its hearty, earthy flavors and, for centuries, they have been developing the cooking techniques that make the most of these ingredients. I decided to take a trip to Tuscany to explore their approach to developing flavor.

11

In Chianti, a region of Tuscany famous for its wine of the same name, the people are passionate and strong. Many of them have a heritage of farming and lots of them enjoy the pleasure of getting into nature to forage for mushrooms or hunt in the thick forests. David Gardner and his wife Catherine moved to Tuscany from Scotland many years ago to open a beautiful hotel called Villa Bordoni. They were taken with the culture and cuisine and have created a place where visitors can experience the "Tuscan life."

Tuscany is a bit unbridled and somewhat wild with its rolling hills and patches of woods. It is at the same time rugged and romantic, and the people there reflect a life very much like that as well. David invited us to join in on an excursion to go hunting for wild boar with some of his friends who belong to a nearby hunt club. Those of us who are not hunters have mental references as to what hunting will be like, and when you start dressing in the proper gear—heavy boots and army green jackets with bright orange vests—it all seems about right. The men smoke cigars and bullshit with each other while they check over all of the guns. The brown and white hunting dogs start going wild in their kennels when the vests go on and the guns are taken out—they know it is almost time for hunting, and this is what they live for. The dogs' excitement and elevated volume is the first hint that this hunt for the wild boar, or *cinghiale* as it is called in Italian, might be a more intense experience than originally expected.

Once the dogs are released from their leashes, everything happens in a flash. Seriously, it goes so fast that disorientation sets in. There are Italian voices resonating through the woods, guns firing in the not-too-distant distance, and when a powerful thunderstorm breaks out in the middle

VILLA BORDONI

Located above the town of Greve in the Chianti Classico region of Tuscany, Villa Bordoni is the fantastic country house hotel owned by veteran restaurateurs David and Catherine Gardner. The 16th century villa has been restored and is now considered one of the most luxurious hotels in Tuscany. Their commitment to pay homage to a Tuscan way of life includes regional wine tastings for guests and cooking lessons from the hotel's experienced Italian chefs.

WILD BOAR

These feral pigs originated in Europe, Asia and Northern Africa and have been introduced to the Americas and Australia. Obtaining the meat from a hunter (or hunting one for yourself) is a nice way to experience the true woodland flavor of an animal that has foraged for its food. However, wild boar are also farm raised and it is fairly easy to obtain the meat from a butcher or online. Some people find the meat of the wild boar to be a bit gamey, so one

DAVID and CATHERINE GARDNER.

VILLA BORDONI, Chianti, ITALY.

The Dining Room at VILLA BORDONI.

of it all, the original hunting scene in your mind's eye gets completely erased. The cinghiale does not lumber along like a domestic pig. These animals are seriously fast and when you see one of these wiry, long-tusked feral pigs headed straight for you, you start looking for a tree to climb! The cinghiale speeds past, the dogs run behind, and the hunters keep shouting and shooting. The entire experience makes you feel incredibly alive—it's the camaraderie and the process of bringing food—and flavor—to the table.

Villa Bordoni's head chef, Francesco Fineo, grew up in this part of Italy, so cooking with ingredients like foraged mushrooms and strong herbs, such as rosemary and sage, as well as cinghiale, is second nature to him. The traditional sauce, dolce forte or "sweet and strong," is a complex sauce that blends strong flavors, such as chili pepper with cocoa, dried fruit and orange zest, and is the perfect sauce to carry the heft of wild boar meat. Francesco's technique displays not just his training, but also his intuition and respect for the ingredients—again, all factors in building flavor. The end result of that recipe is not only a delicious meal, but also one that pays homage to skill, tradition, the hunters, Tuscany and the cinghiale. Somehow, the experience of the day, the smells coming from Francesco's kitchen, even the light in the sky will eventually end up on a plate back home. This is one of the best reasons to travel; food is really a passport to flavor.

MUSHROOMS

of the ways that a cook can reduce that intense flavor is to soak the meat in cold water for 24 hours, changing the water four times within that period. The soak-and-change method will eliminate a lot of the blood in the meat and will reduce the gamey flavor. Also, keep in mind that wild boar does not have nearly as much fat as a domestic pig, so recipes should be adjusted to compensate.

Mushrooms bring very distinct and earthy flavor to all kinds of dishes and sauces. When shopping for mushrooms, make sure they are fresh but not wet or slimy. Also, they should be plump and not drying out. Because a mushroom is like a sponge, washing them with lots of water is not a good thing. Most just need to be brushed off with a soft towel or a brush just before cooking. Most mushrooms respond well to similar cooking techniques but some are more delicate than others. It is easy to discern which ones are big and meaty (and can therefore hold up to more aggressive cooking) and which are more fragile and should be added at the end of a dish.

—**Cultivated mushrooms**, such as the white and brown button mushrooms most often found in the supermarket, are quite different from wild mushrooms. They don't have as intense a flavor as wild varieties have, but they can still be nice if the flavors are intensified by

In PURSUIT of the CINGHIALE.

cooking them long enough to eliminate some of the water that is in them.

–**Shiitake mushrooms** are easy to find year-round because they are actually now being cultivated with good results. They have stems that need to be removed before cooking because they are kind of tough. These stems do hold a lot of flavor, however, and can be used in stocks and soups.

–**Oyster mushrooms and chanterelles** are a bit more delicate in texture. As opposed to cutting these mushrooms, I think the body and shape of the mushrooms remain nice when they are gently broken apart with your hands.

–**Porcini mushrooms**, the prized wild mushroom of Tuscany, are only available in the autumn. In Italy, entire festivals and feasts are held to celebrate their short season, so when you see some in the markets here, take advantage of their appearance. They can be expensive, but when something is available for only a short time, it is cause for celebration. Cook porcini mushrooms with other foods that Tuscans use, such as rosemary, salt and olive oil—simple and amazing.

CINGHIALE DOLCE FORTE.

VILLA BORDONI, Chianti, ITALY.

TUSCAN SUNSET COCKTAIL
24

ARUGULA SALAD WITH BABY TURNIPS,
PINE NUTS AND ORANGE
24

TUSCAN BEAN SOUP
21

PAPPARDELLE WITH WILD BOAR RAGU
AND PORCINI MUSHROOMS
26

CINGHIALE DOLCE-FORTE
27

SOFT POLENTA
28

ROASTED PORK LOIN WITH WILD MUSHROOMS,
GARLIC AND SAGE PAN AU JUS
22

PAN ROASTED DUCK BREAST WITH WILTED ARUGULA
AND DOLCE-FORTE SAUCE
28

TRUFFLE RISOTTO
CHICKEN STOCK
MUSHROOM STOCK
29

CARAMELIZED WHITE CHOCOLATE PANNA COTTA
WITH BLOOD ORANGE MARMALADE
30

TUSCAN BEAN SOUP   SERVES 4 TO 6

Ribollita is a traditional Tuscan soup whose name literally means "reboiled" and was originally made by reheating the minestrone from the previous day. White beans, or cannellini beans as they are known in Italy, are an important staple in Tuscany. This very hearty soup could be simply prepared with just beans, stock and a bit of ham, but innovative cooks use the vegetables they have on hand to make it more special. Here, black kale and chard are combined with herbs, carrots and onions to give lots of color and flavor. A very special trick is to save the hard rind from Parmesan cheese to put in as it cooks—the flavor is very distinct and indicative of that region.

¾   *cup dried cannellini beans, rinsed and soaked overnight, or 1 (15-ounce) can cannellini beans, rinsed and drained*

–   *fine sea salt and freshly ground black pepper*

3   *tablespoons extra virgin olive oil*

4   *ounces thickly sliced prosciutto, diced*

1   *small onion, diced*

1   *cup peeled and diced carrot*

1   *cup diced celery*

2   *garlic cloves, thinly sliced*

4   *cups chicken stock (recipe p. 29)*

1   *small bunch Tuscan black kale (also known as cavolo nero or lacinato kale), sliced crosswise into 1-inch-thick ribbons*

1   *small bunch Swiss chard, stems trimmed, leaves cut in half then sliced into 1-inch-thick ribbons*

3   *plum tomatoes, cored, seeded, and roughly chopped*

2   *thyme sprigs*

3   *tablespoons chopped Italian parsley*

1   *piece Parmesan cheese rind, approx. 3-inch*

GARNISHES

1   *loaf crusty Italian bread, cut into 1-inch cubes*

–   *extra virgin olive oil*

–   *freshly grated Parmesan cheese*

If using dried beans, drain and transfer the beans to a medium pot. Add enough cold water to cover the beans and season with 1 tablespoon of salt. Bring the water to a boil, lower the heat and simmer until tender, about 20 minutes. Drain off most of the cooking liquid, reserving about 2 cups.

Meanwhile, heat the olive oil in a stock pot over medium-high heat. Add the prosciutto, onion, carrot, celery and garlic and cook until lightly caramelized, 6 to 8 minutes. Add the beans, chicken stock, kale, chard, tomatoes, thyme, parsley and Parmesan rind to the pot. Add about 2 cups of water if you're using canned beans. Bring the soup to a simmer and cook until the vegetables are tender, about 30 minutes. Season the soup to taste with salt and pepper.

While the soup is simmering, preheat the oven to 350°F. Place the croutons in a bowl and drizzle a generous amount of olive oil over the bread. Sprinkle the grated Parmesan over the croutons and toss to coat. Place the croutons in a single layer on a baking sheet and bake until they are crisp and golden brown, about 5 to 8 minutes.

Place 4 to 5 croutons in each large soup bowl, ladle the soup over the croutons, and garnish with additional croutons and grated Parmesan cheese as desired. Serve immediately.

ROASTED PORK LOIN WITH WILD MUSHROOMS, GARLIC AND SAGE PAN JUS SERVES 4

This recipe was inspired by my visit to Tuscany and the flavors of the autumn season that were so prevalent while I was there. Searing the pork loin to lock in the juices keeps the meat moist, and the rich pan sauce is made using the drippings from the roasted pork along with the earthy mushrooms. I like to put the garlic cloves in the pan with their skins still on so they sort of roast inside their case; the result is tender roasted garlic.

PORK LOIN AND JUS

- 1 (2-pound) pork loin, trimmed
- 2 tablespoons olive oil
- 1 garlic head, cloves separated, unpeeled
- 3 sage sprigs
- 2 bay leaves, lightly crushed
- ¼ cup dry white wine
- ½ cup chicken stock (recipe p. 29)
- – fine sea salt and freshly ground black pepper

MUSHROOMS

- 12 ounces assorted wild mushrooms, such as morels, porcini, chanterelles and/or oyster mushrooms
- 2 tablespoons canola oil
- 2 tablespoons butter
- 1 small shallot, finely minced
- 2 teaspoons finely minced garlic
- 2 thyme sprigs
- – fine sea salt and freshly ground pepper

Using kitchen string, tie the pork loin once lengthwise and then crosswise, spacing each tie 1 inch apart. Season the pork generously with salt and pepper.

Heat the olive oil in a large sauté pan over medium-high heat. Carefully add the pork loin to the hot pan and sear on all sides until golden, about 6 to 8 minutes. Add the whole garlic cloves. Lower the heat, cover, and continue roasting until medium, about 25 to 30 minutes. Check the doneness of the pork loin by inserting a meat thermometer into the center of the loin; it should register 150°F (it will continue cooking while resting). Transfer the loin to a cutting board and let rest. Reserve the sauté pan.

Meanwhile, prepare the mushrooms: trim and clean all of the mushrooms. Heat the oil and butter in a large sauté pan over medium heat. Add the shallot, garlic and thyme, and cook until the shallot softens, about 3 minutes. Add the mushrooms and sauté until the mushrooms are tender and golden brown, about 5 minutes. Set aside.

Heat the pan (reserved from the pork) over medium heat. Add the sage and bay leaves, and deglaze the pan with the white wine. Simmer to reduce the wine by half, then add the chicken stock and bring to a simmer to lightly reduce again. Add the sautéed mushrooms to the sauce and remove from the heat; set the mushrooms and sauce aside for about 5 minutes to infuse.

Slice the pork loin crosswise into ½-inch-thick slices and lay 3 slices on each of 4 plates. Spoon the mushrooms over and around the pork loin, spoon the jus around, and serve immediately.

WINE PAIRINGS

Pork loin with mushrooms and a garlic-sage pan jus is a simple yet elegant dish that highlights the earthy flavors of the mushrooms. The wine selections spotlight Rhône varietals, which reveal old-world flavors and, therefore, lend some richness to go along with the very grounded flavors of the pork, mushrooms and sage.

BONNY DOON LE CIGARE VOLANT 2004. Santa Cruz, California

When you travel through California, take the opportunity to visit the Bonny Doon Winery in Santa Cruz. The proprietor and mastermind behind these vineyards and winery is Randall Graham, who is a firm believer in biodynamic farming. This type of farming concentrates on natural soil management and pays close attention to the season and the moon phases. It is a very special and old-world way to grow crops. Randall is also considered to be one of the first "Rhône Rangers" of California. "Rhône Ranger" is a moniker given to a California winemaker who focuses on varietals such as Grenache, Syrah, Mourvèdre, Cinsault and Carignane. Le Cigare Volant is based on these varietals, harvested from very old-vine vineyards. Because of this, the wine has more richness and concentration. The level of alcohol is very well integrated and suits a more European palate. The tannins are very delicate and give the wine a good backbone.

COUDOULET DE BEAUCASTEL CÔTES DU RHÔNE 2006. Rhône Valley, France

Wines from the Rhône Valley in France were quite undiscovered by Americans until the past decade when Robert Parker started rating them. Big names, like Côte-Rôtie, Hermitage and Châteauneuf-du-Pape, suddenly came into focus in the international market. The very charming town of Châteauneuf-du-Pape is filled with history, and the wine grown and made here has played an important role in its story.

The Perrin family of Château de Beaucastel, who produces Côtes du Rhône, is known worldwide for their Châteauneuf-du-Pape. Their Coudoulet is sourced from 30 hectares of vines that grow near the famous property, but it does not qualify for the Châteauneuf appellation and is, thus, a Côtes du Rhône. The wine is made up of 30% Grenache, 30% Mourvèdre, 20% Syrah and 20% Cinsault, and has a beautiful lushness in the fruit, the typical delicate earthiness and fine tannins.

TUSCAN SUNSET COCKTAIL   MAKES 1 COCKTAIL

This refreshing cocktail is made with Amaro, which is an Italian herbal liqueur.
The slightly bitter quality that the liqueur possesses blends perfectly with smooth
vodka, rose water and blood orange. These flavors remind me of Tuscany—citrus,
floral and herbal all at the same time.

2   *ounces vodka*
1   *ounce Amaro*
2   *drops rose water*
-   *ice cubes*
1   *ounce blood orange juice*

Stir the vodka, Amaro and rose water in a small pitcher or cocktail shaker
with ice. Fill a rocks glass with ice and strain the vodka mixture into the
glass. Pour the blood orange juice on top and serve immediately.

ARUGULA SALAD WITH BABY TURNIPS, PINE NUTS AND ORANGE   SERVES 4

Arugula literally grows wild on the side of the road in Italy and I love how peppery
and slightly bitter the green is. Baby turnips, sliced thinly, add a bit of earthy sweetness,
and toasted pine nuts with orange segments combine to make a sophisticated salad.

1   *small shallot, minced*
3   *tablespoons red wine vinegar*
-    *fine sea salt and freshly ground*
     black pepper
6   *tablespoons extra virgin olive oil*
8   *ounces baby arugula, washed*
     and trimmed
1   *small bunch baby turnips*
¼   *cup toasted pine nuts, divided*
2   *oranges*

Whisk the shallots and red wine vinegar together in a bowl and season
with some salt and pepper. Drizzle in the olive oil, while whisking, until
fully incorporated.

We don't want to blend the oil into the vinaigrette, just whisk until
combined.

Peel the baby turnips and trim the root ends. Using a sharp knife or man-
doline, slice the turnips very thinly. Combine the turnips, arugula and half
of the pine nuts in another bowl.

Remove the skin and pith from the oranges, and cut between the mem-
branes to remove the segments. Add the segments to the arugula mixture.
Squeeze the juice from the remaining orange pulp into the vinaigrette and
stir to combine.

Gently toss the salad with just enough vinaigrette to coat, and season to
taste with salt and pepper. Divide the salad among 4 bowls, garnish the
salads with the remaining pine nuts and serve immediately.

PAPPARDELLE WITH WILD BOAR RAGU AND PORCINI MUSHROOMS
PAPPARDELLE CON RAGÙ DI CINGHIALE E PORCINI — *adapted from Villa Bordoni*

This recipe, adapted from the one served at Villa Bordoni, is a real homage to the Tuscan hunters who bring the wild boar meat home. Autumn is the perfect time for a hunt, and also for foraging porcini mushrooms. The flavors go perfectly together, and the act of making pasta from scratch is fun and makes the dish very special. Pappardelle is a simple shape of pasta to make, and you will definitely taste the difference in homemade pasta.

SERVES 4

WILD BOAR RAGU

- 3 *tablespoons extra virgin olive oil*
- 1 *pound wild boar shoulder, finely diced*
- – *fine sea salt and freshly ground black pepper*
- 1 *medium onion, diced*
- ½ *pound fresh porcini mushrooms, diced*
- 1 *tablespoon chopped Italian parsley*
- 2 *bay leaves*
- ½ *cup dry red wine*
- 2 *cups canned crushed tomatoes (preferably San Marzano tomatoes)*
- 2 *cups chicken stock (recipe p. 29)*
- 1 *wedge Parmesan cheese for grating*

PAPPARDELLE

- 2 *cups all purpose flour, plus more for dusting*
- 4 *large egg yolks*
- 1 *large whole egg*
- ½ *teaspoon fine sea salt*

Prepare the ragu: To eliminate the gamey flavor of the boar, soak the boar in a large bowl of cold water and refrigerate one day, changing the water several times. Drain well to remove any excess moisture.

Heat the oil in a large heavy pot or a cast-iron Dutch oven over high heat. Add the boar, season with salt and pepper, and sear until nicely browned, about 5 minutes. Reduce the heat to medium. Add the diced onion, porcini mushrooms, parsley and bay leaves and continue cooking, stirring often, until tender, for 5 minutes. Add the red wine and simmer until the mixture is almost dry. Stir in the crushed tomatoes and chicken stock and reduce the heat to low. Simmer the ragu very gently until it is thickened and flavorful, stirring occasionally and adding a little water if the sauce begins to stick, for 1½ to 2 hours. Season the ragu to taste with salt and pepper.

Meanwhile, prepare the pappardelle: Mound 2 cups of flour in the center of a work surface. Make a well in the center of the mound and add the yolks and whole egg to the well. Stir in the salt and slowly work in the flour from the edges until the flour is fully incorporated and a dough forms. Knead the dough, adding more flour as necessary, until silky and smooth. Alternately, all of the ingredients can be put into a food processor fitted with a dough attachment and pulsed until a dough forms. Form the dough into a flat rectangle and wrap tightly in plastic wrap; refrigerate and let rest for at least 20 minutes before using.

Bring a pot of salted water to a boil. Lightly dust a large baking sheet with flour. Flatten and shape the dough into a rectangle that is about ½-inch thick. With the pasta rollers on the widest setting, crank the handle while feeding the dough between the rollers, guiding the dough as it comes out. Fold the dough in half and repeat this process 4 to 5 times, or until the dough is very smooth and silky.

After the last fold and roll, cut the strip of pasta dough in half and cover one half of the dough with a damp towel. Roll the other half of dough through the pasta machine, progressively adjusting the settings on the machine, until the sheet of pasta is slightly thicker than paper. Cut the pasta into 1-inch-wide ribbons and set them on the prepared baking sheet. Repeat the process with the remaining dough.

Just before serving, cook the pappardelle in the large pot of boiling salted water until al dente, about 2 minutes. Drain the pappardelle and transfer it to a platter. Serve with the ragu and freshly grated Parmesan cheese.

CINGHIALE DOLCE-FORTE   *—adapted from Villa Bordoni*

I love the name of this sauce—*dolce-forte* or "sweet-strong." This is a complex sauce that uses ingredients together, such as cinnamon and star anise (the *forte*) with cocoa and dried fruit (the *dolce*), to bring out really big flavor. The addition of orange zest is perfect—not overpowering but just enough to add something unique.

SERVES 4

CINGHIALE

- 2   *pounds wild boar shoulder,*
       cut into large chunks
- 2   *cups dry red wine*
- ½   *cup red wine vinegar*
- 1   *bay leaf*
- 1   *thyme sprig*
- 1   *cinnamon stick*
- ½   *teaspoon grated nutmeg*
- –   *fine sea salt and freshly ground*
       black pepper
- –   *all-purpose flour for dusting*
- ¼   *cup extra virgin olive oil*
- 1   *small onion, finely diced*
- 1   *cup finely diced peeled carrot*
- 1   *cup finely diced celery*
- 2   *cups chicken stock (recipe p. 29)*
- –   *Soft Polenta (recipe p. 28)*

DOLCE-FORTE

- ½   *cup dry red wine*
- ½   *cup prunes*
- ¼   *cup raisins*
- 2   *tablespoons red wine vinegar*
- 1   *tablespoon sugar*
- 1   *cinnamon stick*
- 5   *whole cloves*
- 1   *tablespoon unsweetened cocoa powder*
- 1   *orange*

Combine the boar, red wine, red wine vinegar, bay leaf, thyme, cinnamon stick and nutmeg in a large bowl. Cover the cinghiale and refrigerate overnight or up to 48 hours.

Remove the boar from the marinade, then strain the marinade and set it aside. Season the boar generously with salt and pepper and lightly dust with flour.

Heat the olive oil in a large heavy pot or a cast-iron Dutch oven over high heat. Add just enough pieces of boar to cover the bottom of the pan without crowding them, and sear on all sides until nicely browned, about 8 minutes. Remove the seared boar from the pot and transfer to a bowl. Repeat with the remaining boar pieces. After the last batch of boar is seared, remove the boar from the pot and reduce the heat to medium. Add the diced onion, carrot and celery, and cook until lightly colored, 5 to 7 minutes. Add the strained marinade and simmer until the liquid is reduced by half, about 10 to 15 minutes. Add the chicken stock and bring the liquid to a boil. Return the boar to the pot and stir to combine. Reduce the heat to medium-low so the liquid simmers very gently, cover the pot and braise for about 2 hours, or until the meat is very tender.

Combine the red wine, prunes, raisins, red wine vinegar, sugar, cinnamon stick and cloves in a small saucepan and bring to a boil. Whisk in the cocoa powder. Using a vegetable peeler, shave 1 strip of the orange zest, avoiding the white pith, and add the zest to the prune mixture. Simmer until the mixture thickens slightly, about 5 minutes. Remove the cinnamon stick and cloves from the mixture.

When the stew is done, add the dolce-forte to the stew and simmer briefly until combined, about 5 minutes. Remove the strip of orange zest from the stew and season the stew to taste with salt and pepper. Serve hot with soft polenta.

SOFT POLENTA   SERVES 4

Polenta is made from corn that has been stone ground to a fairly fine grain. Boiled with milk and finished off with butter and Parmesan cheese, polenta makes a beautiful side dish that pairs especially well with hearty meats and sauces.

2   *cups water*
1   *cup whole milk*
–   *fine sea salt and freshly ground black pepper*
¾   *cup polenta*
½   *cup grated Parmesan cheese*
2   *tablespoons butter*

Combine the water, milk and a pinch of salt in a heavy saucepan and bring to a boil over medium heat. Whisk in the polenta gradually to prevent lumps from forming, then reduce the heat to low and cook, stirring occasionally, until creamy, about 20 minutes. Remove the polenta from the heat; cover tightly with foil or a lid, and let sit for 15 minutes.

To serve, stir the Parmesan cheese and butter into the polenta and season to taste with salt and pepper.

PAN ROASTED DUCK BREAST WITH WILTED ARUGULA AND DOLCE-FORTE SAUCE   SERVES 4

The rich, slightly gamey flavor of duck is perfect with the dolce-forte sauce. This sauce combines spices with a bit of dark chocolate and orange zest.

1½   *cups red wine*
1½   *cups red wine vinegar*
¼   *cup sugar*
1   *cinnamon stick*
3   *star anise*
2   *tablespoons whole black peppercorns*
2   *whole cloves*
4   *boneless duck breast halves (6 to 8 ounces each), trimmed*
–   *fine sea salt and freshly ground black pepper*
1   *tablespoon canola oil*
6   *tablespoons unsalted butter*
1   *ounce semisweet chocolate, finely chopped*
10   *ounces arugula*

Combine the red wine, red wine vinegar, sugar, cinnamon stick, star anise, peppercorns and cloves in a non-reactive pot over medium-high heat. Simmer until reduced to ½ cup, about 10-12 minutes. Strain the red wine reduction through a fine-mesh sieve into a small saucepan and set aside.

Preheat the oven to 400°F. Generously season the duck breasts with salt and pepper. Divide the canola oil between two medium sauté pans and heat over medium-high heat. When the pans are hot, gently place two duck breasts, skin side down, in each pan. Lower the heat to medium-low and cook until skin is golden brown and crispy, about 5 to 7 minutes. Discard most of the fat in each pan and place the pans in the oven (do not turn the duck breasts over); continue cooking the duck breasts until they reach medium doneness, about 8 minutes.

While the duck breasts are in the oven, heat the red wine reduction over medium heat and whisk in the butter, one tablespoon at a time, until the butter is fully emulsified (do not allow the sauce to boil). Remove the sauce from the heat and stir in the chocolate. Season to taste with salt and pepper and keep warm.

Remove the duck breasts from the oven and transfer them to a cutting board to rest. Return one of the pans to the stove and add the arugula. Season to taste with salt and pepper and sauté just until the arugula is barely wilted, about 2 to 3 minutes.

Divide the wilted arugula onto the center of 4 plates. Slice each duck into 5 slices and shingle the slices on top of the arugula. Spoon some of the sauce over and around the duck and serve immediately.

TRUFFLE RISOTTO SERVES 4

Learning to cook a proper, creamy risotto is a must. It's not hard—you just have to follow the instructions and stay with it for a little while. I love cooking this way because it means that you are really paying attention to the food. This classic autumn dish combines two very earthy ingredients: mushrooms and truffles. Both are types of fungus that are hunted in the woods. Truffles have a powerful flavor so you don't need much—they are truly precious ingredients.

4   cups chicken stock
    (see recipe below)
2   cups mushroom stock
    (see recipe below)
3   tablespoons olive oil
¼   cup minced onion
1   garlic clove, minced
1½ cups Arborio rice
½   cup dry white wine
½   cup truffle juice, available
    from most gourmet markets
    or from plantin.com
–   fine sea salt and freshly
    ground white pepper
2   tablespoons chopped black truffles
4   ounces freshly grated
    Parmesan cheese
3   tablespoons butter

Bring the chicken stock and mushroom stock to a simmer in separate saucepans; cover and keep warm.

Heat the olive oil in a heavy large saucepan over medium heat. Add the onion and garlic and cook, stirring often, until softened but not colored, about 3 minutes. Stir the rice into the onion and garlic, cooking until the rice turns partially opaque, about 3 minutes. Add the wine and simmer until the wine is reduced and almost dry.

Ladle about 8 ounces of the mushroom stock over the rice and cook, stirring constantly, until the stock is absorbed. Repeat this step, using all of the mushroom stock first, making sure the liquid is absorbed completely after each addition and before adding more, until the rice is tender and creamy, about 15 minutes.

When the rice is just tender, add the truffle juice with the last addition of stock (all of the chicken stock may not be needed). Remove the pan from the heat; season with salt and pepper and stir in the chopped truffles, Parmesan cheese and butter. Serve immediately.

CHICKEN STOCK

MAKES 2 QUARTS

5   pounds chicken backs
3   quarts cold water, approx.

Rinse the chicken well under cold running water and place it in a medium stock pot. Add enough cold water to cover the chicken by 2 inches (about 3 quarts). Bring the water to a boil and then turn the heat down to a low simmer. Simmer the stock for 3 hours. As the stock simmers, use a ladle to carefully skim away any fat and impurities that rise to the surface; discard the fat and impurities.

Remove the stock from the heat and strain it through a fine-mesh sieve, being careful not to press too much of the chicken and sediment into and through the sieve. Degrease the stock again with a ladle. Quickly cool the stock and refrigerate it until ready to use. Scrape off any remaining fat before using.

The stock can be made and refrigerated up to 1 week in advance or stored in the freezer for up to 2 months.

29

MUSHROOM STOCK

MAKES 2 CUPS

5   pounds white button mushrooms
8   cups water, approx.

Clean the mushrooms and place them in a stock pot with 8 cups of water. Bring the water to a boil and simmer over low heat for about 2 hours, or until the liquid is reduced by half. Strain the stock and place it in a clean saucepan. Simmer to reduce the stock by half again.

The stock can be made and refrigerated up to 1 week in advance or stored in the freezer for up to 2 months.

CARAMELIZED WHITE CHOCOLATE PANNA COTTA
WITH BLOOD ORANGE MARMALADE   SERVES 4

This panna cotta is made with rich white chocolate that is actually roasted in the oven for a few minutes. Roasting the white chocolate brings out a totally different flavor that becomes the perfect, rich vehicle for the tart blood orange marmalade that goes on top.

BLOOD ORANGE MARMALADE

- 4   *blood oranges*
- 1½ *cups sugar*
- ½   *teaspoon salt*

PANNA COTTA

- 6   *ounces fine-quality white chocolate, roughly chopped*
- 2   *gelatin sheets*
- ¾   *cup heavy cream*
- ½   *cup whole milk*

For the blood orange marmalade: Scrub the oranges under hot water, then cut them in half. Squeeze the oranges, reserving the juice, and place the juiced rinds in a heavy large saucepan. Add enough water to cover the oranges. Bring the water to a boil over high heat, then drain the water. Cover the oranges with fresh cold water, bring it to a boil and drain again.

Place the boiled orange rinds in a food processor and pulse until they are uniformly chopped. Transfer the chopped oranges to the same pan and stir in the sugar, salt and reserved orange juice. Bring the mixture to a boil, lower the heat to a simmer and let cook for 45 minutes to 1 hour, stirring occasionally. The mixture should be shiny and thick. This recipe will make more than you need but it will keep in the refrigerator for up to 3 months. While the marmalade is cooking, prepare the panna cotta.

For the panna cotta: Preheat the oven to 300°F. Place the chopped white chocolate in a baking dish and place in the oven. After 5 minutes, stir the chocolate, which will have slowly started to brown. Continue to roast the chocolate, stirring occasionally, for another 10 minutes, or until the chocolate has turned a light brown color.

While the chocolate is roasting, soak the gelatin sheets in a bowl of cold water and set aside. Fill a small pot with about 2 inches of water and bring to a simmer. When the chocolate is roasted, transfer it to a medium bowl and place the bowl on top of the small pot of simmering water over low heat. (This "double-boiler" will keep the chocolate warm and make it easier to incorporate.)

In a small saucepan, combine the cream and milk and bring to a boil. Remove the pan from the heat. Remove the gelatin sheets from the water and squeeze to remove the excess water. Add the gelatin sheets to the cream mixture and stir until fully dissolved.

Slowly stir the hot milk mixture into the bowl of white chocolate, making sure the chocolate is fully blended and the mixture has no lumps. Pour the panna cotta mixture into 6- or 8 ounce glass containers or jelly jars. Gently tap the panna cotta to eliminate any air bubbles, cover and refrigerate until set, about 3 hours.

Top each panna cotta with about 2 tablespoons of marmalade and serve.

Chapter 2

STAR INGREDIENTS

Los Gatos, California

GROWING UP IN THE SOUTH OF FRANCE, EATING THE FOOD OF THE REGION AND LEARNING TO COOK FROM MY MOTHER AND GRANDMOTHER GAVE ME A GREAT APPRECIATION FOR INGREDIENTS. Care was always taken in the selection, storage and preparation of the food. I didn't realize it then, but learning early on to choose and care for food was one of the most valuable lessons that I have learned as a chef. While it is important to know how to perform all of the classic techniques—things like knife skills, seasoning, cooking and plating—if you don't start out with good ingredients, the recipe will be a failure. A great dish is dictated by how good the raw materials are.

Finding the source of great ingredients is one of the most important and challenging jobs in a restaurant kitchen. A chef must be able to make good decisions about reputable purveyors, quality products and the best way to use them. Once a great ingredient is found, the proper care must be taken to keep it in good condition and to prepare it with minimal waste. The *garde manger* ("keeping food") station in the kitchen at Le Bernardin is the coldest part of the kitchen and is the place where all the raw fish, cold dishes and salads are prepared and plated. Victor Panora is the garde manger chef here and his job is to make sure that these ingredients are at their very best flavor and presented with precision. Because these plates are usually the first bite that a diner eats at Le Bernardin, it is especially important that the flavors be at their very best.

It is extremely exciting to be in New York City and run the restaurant there. We have the luxury of obtaining really great ingredients from all over the world, but in the city, it is easy to get disconnected from your food source. So it is important to get out, travel, be inspired by nature, and see, touch, taste, smell and learn about your food in a way that can't be replicated in a supermarket. Because so many ingredients come straight to our restaurant, it is intriguing to me when a chef decides to source ingredients in an interesting way. I have a friend in Los Gatos, California, Chef David Kinch, and when I visited the Pacific Coast recently, I stopped by to eat at his incredible restaurant, Manresa, and to see the garden that supplies most of the produce that he uses in the restaurant.

35

Los Gatos, California, is situated on land between the San Francisco Bay and the Pacific Ocean. The town is close to the surfers' mecca, Santa Cruz, and the drive to the ocean proves that this land is farmland—big farmland. David is a surfer and has been all his life. He still enjoys connecting with nature in that way and tries to get out every morning to get in the water and, as he puts it, "cleanse" himself. To get to his favorite cove, we drove down a two-lane highway past sprawling farms and we pulled up next to a gigantic field of Brussels sprouts. The field was so vast that the rows of dark green plants disappeared into the horizon. The Pacific was just on the other side of the rows—incredible. The little sprouts were just beginning to grow on the stalks of the plants and we picked a few off to eat—when they are tiny like that, they are so crisp and slightly sweet.

Love Apple Farm is the name of the garden where master gardener Cynthia Sanberg grows the fruits, herbs and vegetables that stock David's restaurant. David and Cynthia entered the business together with the understanding that the first fruits of the labor would go to Manresa and the rest would be sold to the public. Farming and running a restaurant are both very difficult careers, and when I asked David why he would take on both businesses, he didn't hesitate to explain: "For years I would go to the local farmers' markets to buy produce to use in the restaurant. I found myself standing in a line behind fifteen other chefs buying exactly the same ingredients. Love Apple Farm gives us the opportunity to test new things and grow what we want. It is the most exciting thing I have done for my career in years."

The garden is quite big but is not the sprawling farm that I had seen earlier. It looks quite different because of all the varieties being grown in one place

HEIRLOOM VEGETABLE

The definition of what true heirloom vegetables are is hotly debated, but most agree that for a plant to be an heirloom, it must come from seed and plant stock dated before 1951. After World War II, industrial farming and seed hybridization became widespread. The reasons for this seemed harmless to the general public—the hybrids being bred were easy to grow and pest and disease resistant. Some things, like very distinct flavor, are lost and the threat of the varietal gene pool becoming too shallow is very real. New interest in saving seeds and growing heirloom varieties is happening among commercial farmers and home gardeners alike. It is interesting to compare colors and flavors, breeding lots of inspiration for how to use them in new recipes. There are great sources for seeds and advocates of saving heirloom varieties online. www.seedsavers.org www.seedsofchange.com

David's morning ritual.

KITCHEN GARDENS

Kitchen gardens are a great way to incorporate some homegrown food into your menus. The act of placing a seed or seedling in a pot, taking care of it, and then incorporating it into a recipe is a demonstration of the cycle that keeps us all going. Because we usually depend on others for all the hard work (taking care of plants and animals, nourishing them, harvesting, packaging and selling our food) we are not often reminded of the efforts required to put healthy food on a plate. Having your own tomatoes in the garden or basil growing in the window is a satisfying feeling. Achieving this is as easy as buying a potted herb and placing it in your window or digging up space in your backyard or community garden. Introduce children to how plants grow and where our food comes from by showing them how to plant a seed and watch it sprout and grow. It is a very profound way to connect yourself and others to food and nature.

37

together. Tucked away in a residential area, Love Apple Farm is bursting with all kinds of fruits, vegetables, herbs and laying hens for eggs. They make very good use of their land and they maintain the garden using biodynamic principles. It is a challenge to commit to this type of farming but the payoff is big. Farming in this way is self-sustaining and essentially means that just as much attention is paid to the quality and health of the soil as is paid to the vegetables themselves. Lots of trial and error goes into gardening and, because they are trying to grow so many kinds of rare and heirloom varieties, it means that there will be some great success and some failure. Gardening is very much like developing new recipes—all of it is a learning experience.

It was interesting to see all of the different vegetables, like the heirloom tomatoes with their strange colors, shapes and sizes. They had interesting and descriptive names such as Top Sirloin, which is big and meaty, or Green Zebra and Cherokee Purple. There were all kinds of squash and pumpkins growing, including one that I remember from France called *potimarron*. Nasturtium flowers were trailing out onto the garden paths and the autumn colors were so abundant and inspiring. Being there helped me understand how this has become such an important part of David's business. He told me, "The garden writes the menu now. We have this great produce and we have to use it. Our job is not to lose the produce in the kitchen. The responsibility is to present these beautiful products and, many times, that means to back away and use very simple cooking methods. When we have new cooks start at the restaurant, the first thing we do is have them come to the garden. Once they understand how things grow, look and taste in the garden and what goes into the process, it changes their perspective completely."

Finally, sitting down to eat at Manresa, it is very clear how David's work and his vision are played out on the plate. Literally, his garden and even the morning spent at the ocean came to the table in different forms. A gorgeous yellow-orange soup made from the potimarron pumpkin was served with a quenelle of nasturtium flower ice cream and toasted pumpkin seeds. The ice cream melted into the soup and changed each bite, adding the peppery flavor of the flowers and adjusting the temperature of the soup at the same time. It was perfection. Another dish turned out to be Chef Kinch's homage to an autumn tidal pool—a shallow puddle of delicious clear broth filled with clams,

"THE GARDEN WRITES the MENU."

abalone, urchin and seaweed. One of David's signature dishes is called "Into the Garden" and is a composition of sometimes 60 or 70 different ingredients. Assembled delicately, using long tweezers, perfect tiny sprouts, shoots, leaves, herbs and single shavings or slices of just-picked raw vegetables are dressed in nothing more than a foam made from the spun juices of the vegetables used. An "edible soil," made from finely crushed roasted chicory root, dehydrated potato, parsnip and toasted almonds, is sprinkled onto the plate. The result is a work of art and is, as David describes it, "like holding a mirror up to the garden on that very day." It takes restraint and a lot of confidence as a chef to allow the ingredients to be the star. He is elevating every component with the ultimate respect for these star ingredients.

Highlighting one really perfect ingredient is a good way to plan a menu at home too. At Le Bernardin, as well as at my home, the focus of any recipe is to make one beautiful ingredient the star of the plate and let the other ingredients enhance that star. A good example is to take something like a perfect salmon fillet, season it simply with salt and pepper and sear it simply in a hot pan with some light oil. When the fish is great (and you should never buy fish that is not great) you don't need to do much to it. Cooked properly and dressed minimally, the fish will shine through. I also like to put something fresh and seasonal on the plate that makes the main ingredient stand out. For example, pairing the salmon with bright green pea shoots fresh from the farmers' market brings out all the wonderful qualities of the salmon even more. Allow what you find, your knowledge of that flavor, and perhaps a good memory to dictate how you use ingredients. For me, walking through the garden and seeing the ocean and all of the life that grows in and around it—even the wild plants on the side of the road—will be inspiration that I will use in some way.

"INTO THE GARDEN"

SANTA CRUZ, California.

Goat ROCK BEACH, SONOMA COAST, California.

CRAB-STUFFED ZUCCHINI FLOWERS
WITH MUSTARD BUTTER SAUCE   SERVES 4

These large yellow blossoms are the flowers that form on the fruit of the zucchini plant. They have a beautiful color, a delicate texture and a slight peppery taste. Filled with a creamy mixture of sweet crabmeat, they are steamed and then dressed with a creamy mustard butter sauce.

ZUCCHINI FLOWERS

8   *ounces Peekytoe crabmeat*
2   *tablespoons crème fraîche*
1   *lemon, zested and juiced*
1   *tablespoon thinly sliced chives*
–   *fine sea salt and freshly ground white pepper*
–   *piment d'Espelette*
12   *large zucchini flowers, stamens removed*

MUSTARD BUTTER SAUCE

1   *tablespoon water*
6   *tablespoons unsalted butter*
½   *tablespoon Dijon mustard*
½   *tablespoon whole grain mustard*
–   *fine sea salt and freshly ground white pepper*
1   *tablespoon thinly sliced chives*

Combine the crabmeat, crème fraîche, lemon juice and zest, and chives in a mixing bowl. Season to taste with salt, white pepper and piment d'Espelette. Using a small spoon or a piping bag, gently stuff each zucchini flower three-quarters full with the crab mixture.

Bring the water to a boil in a heavy small saucepan over medium heat and whisk in the butter 1 tablespoon at a time until the all of the butter is emulsified. Whisk in both mustards and season to taste with salt and pepper. Set the butter sauce aside and keep warm.

Place a large pot filled with 2 inches of water over high heat and bring to a boil. Place the stuffed zucchini flowers in a steamer insert, then set the steamer in the pot. Cover and steam until the crab filling is hot, about 3 minutes.

Place 3 zucchini flowers on each of 4 plates. Stir the chives into the mustard butter sauce, spoon the sauce over and around the stuffed flowers and serve immediately.

HEIRLOOM TOMATO SALAD
WITH BLACK GARLIC AND WHITE BALSAMIC   SERVES 4

Choosing an assortment of heirloom tomatoes—those of all shapes and colors—will result in a very beautiful and interesting salad. Heirloom varieties are breeds that have not been hybridized and retain their original flavor and texture. Another interesting ingredient in this dish is the black garlic, which is a preserved, Korean-style of garlic. It is very dense, with a sweet yet earthy quality.

1   *head black garlic (see note)*
1   *pint cherry tomatoes*
1½   *pounds heirloom tomatoes, assorted sizes, shapes and colors*
–   *fine sea salt and freshly ground black pepper*
¼   *cup torn fresh basil leaves*
3   *tablespoons white balsamic vinegar*
6   *tablespoons extra virgin olive oil*

Note: Black garlic is preserved garlic from Korea; it is available at specialty food markets or from Kalustyans.com.

Separate and peel the fermented black garlic cloves. Cut the cloves into very thin slices, dipping your blade into warm water after each slice, and set aside.

Cut the cherry tomatoes in half. Core the heirloom tomatoes and cut the smaller tomatoes into wedges. Cut the larger tomatoes in half, then slice them into ¼-inch-thick slices.

Arrange the tomatoes on a large platter. Season the tomatoes with salt and pepper. Scatter the sliced garlic and torn basil over the tomatoes, and drizzle the white balsamic vinegar and olive oil over the salad. Serve immediately.

47

SMOKED SALMON CARPACCIO
WITH TOASTED BRIOCHE AND TOBIKO —*adapted from Le Bernardin*

This elegant appetizer is a direct adaptation from one of the most popular dishes we serve at Le Bernardin. The technique of pounding the salmon very thin and then cutting it into shapes makes it easy to fashion it into something special. Tobiko is a very flavorful flying fish roe (caviar) and it brings a good amount of flavor and salt.

SERVES 4

10 *ounces smoked salmon, sliced very thin (8 slices)*
4 *slices brioche, each about ¼-inch thick*
3 *tablespoons crème fraîche*
4 *ounces tobiko (see note)*

Special Equipment
– *6-inch round ring mold*
– *3-inch round cutter*

Note: Tobiko is flying fish roe of Japanese origin; it is available at seafood stores and Japanese markets.

Lay a large sheet of plastic wrap onto a work surface. Lay the salmon slices in pairs, side by side, on the plastic, leaving about 1 inch of space around each pair. Cover the slices with another sheet of plastic wrap. Using a kitchen mallet or the back of a heavy skillet, gently pound the salmon slices until they are thin and even.

Place the 6-inch ring mold on top of one of the salmon portions so the two slices meet in the center of the mold. Using a sharp knife and the ring mold as a template, cut through the salmon and both layers of plastic, creating a portion of two equal-sized half circles. Repeat this step with the remaining portions of pounded salmon slices.

Preheat the toaster oven to broil. Cut 4 slices of brioche with the 3-inch round cutter. Arrange the brioche slices on a tray and lightly toast in the broiler until golden brown. Remove from the toaster and let cool.

Spread a small dollop of crème fraîche onto each toast and place each toast in the center of a plate. Holding one portion of the pounded salmon flat on your hand, remove the plastic from the top side, then invert and place it on top of the toast. Using the plastic on top of the salmon, gently adjust the centering, then remove the plastic and separate the two slices in the middle to expose the toast. Spoon 1 ounce of tobiko into the opening, covering the exposed toast and crème fraîche. Repeat with the remaining toasts, salmon and tobiko. Serve immediately.

PUMPKIN SOUP WITH SPICED PUMPKIN SEEDS
AND NASTURTIUMS —*adapted from Manresa*

This autumn recipe is adapted from a delicious soup by my friend, chef David Kinch of Manresa restaurant located in Los Gatos, California. The creamy orange pumpkin soup is garnished with toasted pumpkin seeds and peppery yellow and orange nasturtium flowers.

SERVES 4-6

SOUP

2   *tablespoons unsalted butter*
½   *cup sliced onion*
½   *garlic clove, chopped*
2½ *pounds pumpkin or butternut squash,*
    peeled, seeded, and diced
4   *cups chicken stock (recipe p. 29)*
¾   *cup heavy cream*
1   *Italian parsley sprig*
1   *thyme sprig*
½   *tablespoon whole black peppercorns*
1   *bay leaf*
–   *fine sea salt and freshly ground white pepper*

GARNISHES

–   *spiced pumpkin seeds (recipe follows)*
–   *nasturtium flowers*

SPICED PUMPKIN SEEDS
MAKES ABOUT ½ CUP

1   *tablespoon butter*
½   *cup shelled raw pumpkin seeds*
¼   *teaspoon cayenne pepper*
¼   *teaspoon ground toasted coriander*
¼   *teaspoon ground toasted cumin*
–   *fine sea salt and freshly ground white pepper*

Melt the butter in a large pot over medium heat. Add the sliced onion and garlic and sauté until translucent, about 3 minutes. Add the diced squash and sauté until softened, about 10 minutes. Cover with the chicken stock and bring to a simmer. Cook until the squash is tender, about 30 minutes.

Working in batches, puree the soup in a blender until satiny smooth. Pass the soup through a fine chinois to remove any remaining lumps. Return the soup to the pot and add the cream. Bring the soup to a simmer.

Wrap the parsley, thyme, peppercorns and bay leaf in cheesecloth and tie closed with kitchen string. Add the herb bundle to the simmering soup and infuse for 10 minutes. Remove the bundle and season the soup to taste with salt and pepper.

Ladle the soup into bowls and garnish with the spiced pumpkin seeds and nasturtium petals.

Melt the butter in a sauté pan over medium heat. Add the pumpkin seeds, cayenne, coriander, and cumin and toast the pumpkin seeds until they are golden brown, stirring frequently, about 5 to 7 minutes.

49

SEARED SALMON WITH SAUTÉED PEA SHOOTS AND GINGER-SOY VINAIGRETTE   SERVES 4

Salmon is one of the most popular fish in America. It is very easy to make salmon in a delicious and simple way at home. Start by choosing the freshest fish available and sear it in a very hot pan for a short time. The combination of salmon, fresh peas and pea shoots creates an easy, fresh and beautiful dish.

GINGER-SOY VINAIGRETTE

¼   *cup olive oil*

3   *tablespoons fresh lime juice*

2   *tablespoons soy sauce*

1   *tablespoon grated peeled fresh ginger*

½   *teaspoon minced garlic*

–   *fine sea salt and freshly ground black pepper*

PEA SHOOTS

1   *tablespoon canola oil*

8   *cups baby pea shoots (if not available, use adult pea shoot tops)*

¼   *cup shelled and blanched English peas*

2   *teaspoons minced peeled fresh ginger*

1   *teaspoon minced garlic*

–   *fine sea salt and freshly ground black pepper*

SALMON

1   *(2 pound) salmon fillet, skin and bones removed, fillet cut into 8 slices (each about 1-inch thick)*

2   *tablespoons canola oil*

–   *fine sea salt and freshly ground pepper*

For the vinaigrette, stir all of the ingredients together in a bowl; season to taste with salt and pepper and set aside.

For the pea shoots, heat the canola oil in a large sauté pan over high heat. Add the pea shoots and peas and cook just until the pea shoots are wilted, about 3 minutes. Add the ginger, garlic and 2 tablespoons of the vinaigrette and toss to combine. Season to taste with salt and pepper, remove the pan from the heat and set aside.

For the salmon, preheat a griddle or plancha on high heat until very hot. Season the salmon slices on both sides with salt and pepper and brush them with canola oil. Sear the salmon on the griddle or plancha until golden brown and crusted, about 1½ minutes on each side. A metal skewer can be easily inserted into the salmon when it is done, and when the skewer is left in the salmon for 5 seconds it feels just warm when touched to the lip.

To serve, divide the pea shoots and peas among 4 plates. Place 2 salmon slices on top of the pea shoots on each plate, slightly off-center from each other. Spoon the vinaigrette around the pea shoots and serve immediately.

WINE PAIRINGS

The dressing that tops the salmon with peas and pea shoots in this recipe has soy sauce, ginger and some lime in it. Even though these flavors can be somewhat tricky to pair wine with, here, they work well with the hearty salmon and the soy sauce adds a little depth to the fresh, green taste of the pea shoots creating a very balanced dish. The wines chosen are very food friendly and their richness rounds out the flavors when paired together.

ROUSSANNE, QUPÉ 2007

Roussanne is a white wine grape originally grown in the Rhone wine region in France. The aroma of Roussanne usually has a flowery tone to its base that often delivers rich and full-bodied wines. Qupé winery is certainly one of the leading Roussanne producers in California. The Roussanne is from the cool Santa Maria Valley where it finds long ripening seasons and is able to keep higher acid levels. Given a 12 month oak aging, the wine is soft and round combined with characteristic richness.

PINOT NOIR, CALERA. Central Coast, California

Pinot Noir is a very moody varietal, meaning it has phases where the wine tastes great and then the wine is completely closed up and unapproachable. In California, the winemakers take a different approach than the French, and of course the land is different so the wine tends to be a little less "moody." The result is wine that is more fruit forward and softer in tannins. The style of Pinot Noir from Calera is always clean and with a good amount of complexity in their wines. The delicate richness of this Pinot is responsible for this pairing with the salmon.

ROASTED LEG OF LAMB SERVES 6

Leg of lamb is one of the most flavorful meats, and it only needs some garlic, herbs, salt and pepper to make it delicious. Lamb is better cooked medium; use an instant-read meat thermometer to ensure you don't overcook it.

1 (4-pound) bone-in leg of lamb
2 garlic cloves
2 rosemary sprigs
3 thyme sprigs
– fine sea salt and freshly ground black pepper
3 tablespoons canola oil
2 tablespoons butter
– Market Vegetables with Ravigote Vinaigrette (recipe p. 53)

Preheat the oven to 450°F. Heat a large roasting pan in the oven. Meanwhile, cut the garlic cloves into ¼-inch-thick slices. Make incisions in the leg of lamb and insert the garlic slices and small sprigs of rosemary and thyme into the incisions. Season the lamb thoroughly with salt and pepper.

Add the canola oil to the hot roasting pan and carefully place the lamb in the roasting pan. Roast the lamb in the oven to sear it on all sides, turning as necessary, 15 to 20 minutes. Reduce the oven temperature to 350°F. Add the butter to the roasting pan and continue roasting the lamb, basting frequently, for 35 to 45 minutes. When the lamb is done, a meat thermometer should register 140°F for medium when inserted into the thickest part of the lamb (the lamb will continue cooking while it's resting).

Remove the lamb from the oven and let rest for at least 20 minutes. Using a large sharp knife, slice the lamb against the grain and serve with the market vegetables.

MARKET VEGETABLES WITH RAVIGOTE VINAIGRETTE   SERVES 4

This dish utilizes whatever seasonal vegetables are available in the market. The idea is to see what your local farmers have grown and pick things that will complement each other and make a beautiful dish. The ravigote vinaigrette is a classic French combination of sherry vinegar, shallots, cornichons and hard-boiled egg.

MARKET VEGETABLES

- 1   *ear of corn, shucked*
- ¼   *pound green beans, ends trimmed*
- ½   *pound baby squash with flowers*
- 1   *small bunch leeks, ends trimmed*
- 1   *small fennel bulb, cored and sliced*
- 1   *small bunch baby turnips,*
      peeled and quartered
- 1   *small bunch baby carrots,*
      peeled and halved lengthwise
- –   *sea salt*

RAVIGOTE VINAIGRETTE

- 3   *tablespoons aged sherry vinegar*
- 1   *teaspoon Dijon mustard*
- 5   *tablespoons canola oil*
- 5   *tablespoons extra virgin olive oil*
- –   *fine sea salt and freshly ground*
      black pepper
- 1   *large egg, hard boiled, yolk and*
      white separated and chopped
- 2   *teaspoons finely diced cornichons*
- 1   *teaspoon capers, finely chopped*
- 1   *teaspoon chopped fresh Italian parsley*
- 1   *teaspoon chopped fresh tarragon*
- 1   *teaspoon finely diced shallot*
- 1   *teaspoon finely sliced fresh chives*

Bring 3 pots of water to a boil over high heat and add salt to each pot. Drop the ear of corn into one pot, the green beans into the second pot and the fennel into the third pot. Cook until crisp-tender, about 3 minutes for the corn and 4 minutes for the green beans and fennel. Using a strainer, remove the vegetables from the boiling water and submerge them in an ice water bath to stop them from cooking.

Repeat with the baby squash, leeks, turnips and carrots, cooking the turnips and carrots together and the squash and leeks in separate pots, for 3 to 4 minutes each. Cut the corn kernels off the cob and halve or quarter the green beans and leeks, depending on their size.

Whisk the sherry vinegar and Dijon mustard in a large bowl to blend. Slowly whisk in the canola oil and olive oil. Adjust the seasonings and season to taste with salt and pepper. Gently mix the egg whites and yolks, cornichons, capers, parsley, tarragon, shallot and chives into the vinaigrette.

Arrange the vegetables equally on 6 plates and spoon the vinaigrette over the vegetables. Serve immediately.

WHITE ASPARAGUS WITH ANCHOVY-HERB BUTTER SERVES 4

White asparagus is the same plant as green asparagus but the shoots are kept completely
covered while they grow, which prevents photosynthesis (the process that makes plants green).
The result is a creamy, white shoot with a sweeter, more delicate flavor.

ANCHOVY-HERB BUTTER

¼ *cup chervil leaves*
¼ *cup Italian parsley leaves*
¼ *cup sliced chives*
3 *tablespoons extra virgin olive oil*
1 *tablespoon sliced tarragon leaves*
1 *tablespoon capers*
3 *anchovy fillets*
1 *small shallot, thinly sliced*
1 *small garlic clove, thinly sliced*
– *pinch of cayenne pepper*
6 *ounces very soft unsalted butter*
2 *tablespoons fresh lemon juice*
– *fine sea salt and freshly ground
    white pepper*

WHITE ASPARAGUS

20 *stalks of white asparagus,
     peeled and ends trimmed*
 – *fine sea salt*

For the anchovy-herb butter, combine all of the ingredients except the
butter and lemon juice in a blender and blend until smooth. Add the
butter and lemon juice and gently blend, being careful not to over-
process the butter. Season to taste with salt and pepper.

Cook the asparagus in a large pot of boiling salted water until very
tender, about 8 to 10 minutes. Remove the pot from the heat and allow
the asparagus to rest in the liquid while the sauce is being prepared.
Remove the asparagus from the water and place on a paper towel to
remove the excess water.

Arrange 5 asparagus stalks, tips pointing in the same direction, on each
of 4 plates. Spoon the anchovy-herb butter over the asparagus and
serve immediately.

ROASTED CARROTS WITH BABY PEA SHOOTS
AND CURRY VINAIGRETTE SERVES 4

Roasting carrots brings out their natural sugars and, at the same time, imparts an earthy quality to the vegetable. Pea shoots are the green leaves and tendrils of a pea plant and provide a fresh crunch, while the curry vinaigrette adds an exotic note.

2 *pounds baby carrots,*
   assorted shapes and colors
4 *tablespoons extra virgin olive oil*
– *fine sea salt and freshly ground*
   black pepper
½ *cup canola oil*
1 *teaspoon Madras curry powder*
1 *teaspoon ground toasted coriander*
1 *teaspoon ground toasted cumin*
½ *teaspoon dried hot chili flakes*
3 *tablespoons white balsamic vinegar*
1 *tablespoon minced shallot*
1 *teaspoon grated ginger*
2 *cups baby pea shoots*

Preheat the oven to 350°F. Wash the baby carrots, trim off the tops, then pat the carrots dry. Place the carrots in a single layer on a roasting pan, drizzle the olive oil over the carrots and season with salt and pepper. Roast the carrots until they are tender, 25 to 35 minutes, stirring every 10 minutes.

Meanwhile, stir the canola oil, curry powder, coriander, cumin and chili flakes in a small bowl to blend and set aside for at least 10 minutes to let the flavors infuse. (The curry oil can be made up to 1 week ahead and kept in the refrigerator until ready to use.) Whisk the vinegar, shallot and ginger in a medium bowl and season with salt and pepper. Slowly drizzle in the curry oil, while whisking constantly, until fully combined; adjust the seasonings to taste.

Remove the carrots from the oven and spoon about 3 tablespoons of the curry vinaigrette over the carrots, gently tossing to coat evenly. Divide the carrots among 4 plates, top with the pea shoots and drizzle more of the curry vinaigrette around the plate. Serve immediately.

BLACKBERRY TOMATO CRUMBLE   SERVES 4

Cherry tomatoes are sweet and acidic, just like berries, so Michael Laiskonis, the pastry chef
at Le Bernardin, put the two together to create this innovative dessert. Macerating the tomatoes
and berries in a syrup infused with basil and tarragon, then serving them with a sweet streusel,
blurs the lines between sweet and savory in a brilliant way.

CRUMBLE

½   cup almond flour
½   cup all-purpose flour
¼   cup unsalted butter, cold,
    cut into small cubes
4   tablespoons granulated sugar
2   tablespoons light brown sugar
–   pinch of fine sea salt

FRUIT

1   pint small grape tomatoes
1   cup granulated sugar
1   cup water
1   cup fresh basil leaves,
    loosely packed
3   tarragon sprigs, divided
1   lemon, zested and juiced
1   vanilla bean, split lengthwise
1   pint fresh blackberries
–   lemon zest strips, for garnish

For the crumble, stir all the ingredients in a large bowl until it forms a pebble-
like consistency. Cover and chill for 1 hour. Meanwhile, preheat the oven to
325°F and line a baking sheet with parchment paper.

Gently spread the crumble mixture onto the prepared baking sheet and bake
for 10 to 15 minutes or until the crumble is golden brown. Allow the crumble
to cool, then break the crumble into smaller pieces, if necessary.

For the fruit, bring a medium pot of water to a rapid boil over high heat. Carefully drop the tomatoes into the boiling water and cook for just 5 to 10 seconds,
then strain and immediately plunge the tomatoes into a small bowl of ice water.
Drain the tomatoes and peel each one using a small knife.

Combine the sugar and 1 cup of water in a small saucepan and bring to a boil.
Remove from the heat. Stir in the basil, 2 tarragon sprigs and the lemon zest
and juice from 1 lemon. Scrape the seeds from the vanilla bean into the syrup,
then add the bean to the syrup. Cover and set aside to infuse the syrup and allow it to cool. Strain the syrup through a fine-mesh sieve.

Thoroughly rinse the blackberries and dry them on a paper towel. Place the
berries and peeled tomatoes in a small bowl and cover with the infused syrup.
Chill and macerate for at least 1 hour. Drain the fruit and reserve the syrup.

Arrange the fruit in 4 shallow serving dishes and top each with a spoonful
of the reserved syrup, then top each serving with 3 to 4 tablespoons of the
crumble. Garnish with the leaves from the remaining tarragon sprig and strips
of lemon zest. Serve immediately.

Chapter 3

FARMING THE SEA

Marshall, California

FRESH OYSTERS SERVED SIMPLY ON A BED of ICE with LEMON.

AT LE BERNARDIN, THE FOCUS OF THE MENU IS SEAFOOD. Fish and shellfish are all extremely perishable and once caught or harvested, the products must be brought to land and sent to market or directly to the buyers as soon as possible. Every day, about 2,000 pounds of extremely fresh seafood comes into the receiving area at Le Bernardin. Immediately, Fernando Uruchima, the porter at the restaurant, checks the fish for quality and then turns them over to Justo Thomas, who begins to butcher the fish. The shellfish—oysters, clams, langoustine, urchin, mussels, scallops and lobsters—are cleaned and checked, then put on ice and stored in the cooler or processed for the day's service. Over 200 oysters are sold every day at the restaurant, and once an order comes in, the oysters are shucked right then, carefully placed on a bed of ice and sent to the dining room.

People living near the sea have eaten oysters for thousands of years. They are amazing creatures but are at the mercy of the correct growing conditions and healthy waters. Some of the world's great oyster-producing regions have been destroyed by pollution or over-harvesting, but we are learning how to manage some of these conditions now and oysters have a bright future.

Lots of residents and visitors to San Francisco are familiar with the Hog Island Oyster Company because of their restaurant located on the docks of the beautifully restored Ferry Building in the heart of the city. Still functioning as a hub of transportation, business people commute from towns all over the greater Bay Area by ferry and pass through the building every day. The Ferry Building outpost of the Hog Island Oyster Company has been open for just a few years, but marine biologists John Finger and Terry Sawyer, co-owners of the company, have been sustainably farming oysters since 1983 in the Tomales Bay area of northern California.

Traveling pre-dawn means thick fog, and the occasional sounding of a foghorn in the distance reminds you that there is a dangerous shoreline close by and reinforces how wild the landscape and climate are here. Eventually, and quite quickly, the fog lifts as the first glimmers of light shine from just under the horizon and the sky takes on an orange-pink glow. Pulling into the oyster-shell-paved area of a boat dock, I see several men in hip waders who have already been working for a couple of hours.

61

The Tomales Bay is a 6,800-acre estuary that is part of the Point Reyes National Seashore. Hog Island is a tiny speck of land in that watershed, and it is in the waters near Hog Island where these oystermen have made their beds. I met John Finger on the dock that morning and he agreed to take me out onto the bay and into the oyster beds to teach me how oysters grow and what makes these oysters so good. On the boat, heading toward a section of their 160-acre farm, John explains, "Shellfish are constantly filtering water through their open shells as they lie on the sea floor. This water is very clean and full of nutrients, which means the oysters are healthy and, in turn, they help to keep the water clean by constantly filtering it. It's a symbiotic relationship."

The water is pristine and ahead there are rows of what looks like barrels floating just on the surface. When we are close, the boat motor is turned off and we jump into the knee-deep water. Once I am in the oyster beds, I see that the things that looked like barrels are actually mesh cages that house the seed oysters—very small young oysters—as they grow. Once they grow to a certain size, the seed oysters will be moved to large mesh bags that stay just below the water's surface. They stay in these metal bags until they are big enough to harvest. Looking into the bags, it is easy to see them because the water is so clear. I can tell they are slightly open—filtering the water and picking up essential nutrients. It is easy to reach in and pull an oyster out to get a closer look and to crack one open to eat. The oyster is plump and delicious and truly tastes of the area itself: clean, salty and sweet all at the same time.

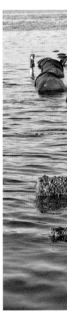

Walking through the beds, I notice bright green seaweed growing on top of the cages. It looks familiar and, just as I thought, John explains that it is sea lettuce and pulls some up for me to look at. John seems a little surprised when I immediately put it in my mouth to taste. He admits that while he knew that it was edible, he doesn't regard it as something that might be good to eat. Tasting a few different pieces, I realize that the smaller pieces are tastier and the big pieces are a little tough. I am intrigued though and, in my mind, I could really taste this in some kind of salad with a Caesar-like dressing. We gather some to take back to the shore so that I can work it into a recipe. I am pretty sure John thought I was a little crazy.

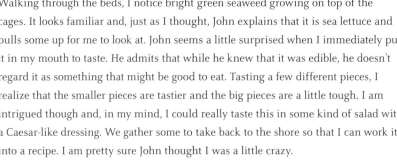

The Hog Island Oyster Company has a very interesting and functional base camp on the beach in the tiny town of Marshall, California. This base camp is where the Pacific, Kumamoto, and Atlantic oysters grow, along with Manila clams and mussels,

ETHICALLY PURCHASING SEAFOOD

There are lots of conflicting reports and information about the right way to purchase seafood. Buzz phrases, like wild-caught, farm-raised, over-fished, line, net and seasonal, float around and make it confusing. Respected chefs, markets and fishmongers can help consumers know what is good to buy and when. Because fish, and really all food, is a reflection of its surroundings, the same type of fish from various places can taste totally different. That is one reason you will often see the provenance of a product displayed on a menu. Just like wine, terroir is evident in food, and wild-caught fish is really the best because it is seasonal and reflects its history. At one time, farm-raised seafood was completely frowned upon for different reasons, but as time goes on and farm practices change, the information is updated. At Le Bernardin, we have found some very good farm-raised smoked salmon that we use with farm-raised caviar for one of our most popular dishes. And then there are the amazing shellfish from Hog Island Oyster Company.

The point is that updated education is the key. Forge a relationship with a seafood professional and keep an eye on some good sources of information. There are sustainable seafood guides online and smart phone apps that can help.

SEED OYSTER BARREL CAGES.

and are brought in, rinsed, sorted and kept in pristine holding tanks, ready to be taken into the Bay Area's restaurants and bars. The company has also set up picnic tables right on the beach, allowing travelers to pull over and enjoy fresh oysters right where they are being harvested. It is a wonderful way to connect with a culture, the landscape and its food in a manner that forces you to truly consider the source.

Once back on shore, John and I, along with Terry Sawyer, open some of the morning's harvest. They taught me to make their version of a classic mignonette called "Hog Wash" (*recipe p. 72*), which is a flavorful mix of vinegar, shallot, jalapeño and cilantro. I also put together a salad using the sea lettuce that we brought back, mixed with some baby bok choy, bell pepper, lemon, scallions and freshly shucked oyster meat (*recipe p. 71*). Because the sea lettuce salad was something that we just sort of threw together, there was a chance that it might not have worked; but being in contact with nature and in that surrounding, it is important to let the inspiration of the place take over. The salad was actually delicious and went very well with the fresh oysters and sparkling wine we opened. When I got there that morning, it was cold and very early, and I was a little bit grumpy. But going out on the boat, surrounded by water with everything so beautiful around you—and to see the oysters in their element—was such a powerful experience. It created immediate inspiration.

Back in New York, at the restaurant, we have weekly meetings with all of the chefs and sous chefs to discuss the menu and anything interesting that we might have found to taste and try to work into the recipes. Because we focus on seafood, the ocean and sea life are a constant source of inspiration. The chefs work with all kinds of seaweed and are familiar with its textures and flavors, but we have never served any sea lettuce like I saw in the Tomales Bay. It was fun to tell them the story of gathering it and mixing it with the oyster-Caesar dressing to create a true surprise for the people who work around that sea lettuce every day. I don't know if we will be able to find a source for the lettuce, but that is part of our job—to find the inspiration and then see it through to the plate.

SHUCKING OYSTERS

Opening oysters properly takes practice. A proper oyster knife is necessary and, until you are very good at it, wearing a glove or using a thick towel to guard your non-knife-wielding hand is a good idea. It is important to hold the oyster with the "bowl" or "cupped" side down. Slide the point of the knife into a place near the back of the hinge of the shell, and then twist the knife one way and then the other way until the shell starts to give. Once the crack gets wider, you can then insert the knife a little more and separate the two shells. Try not to dig the knife into the meat of the oyster. Once the top of the shell is off, take care not to spill the "liquor" that is inside the oyster—this flavorful liquid is the remaining seawater that keeps the oyster alive and plump. Gently slide the knife under the oyster meat to cut the muscle that attaches it to the shell. The oyster is now ready to be placed on ice for service or eaten immediately.

MARSHALL, California, home of Hog Island OYSTER Co.

SHUCKING OYSTERS with JOHN.

TASTING OYSTERS

Oysters, like all regional food products, are a reflection of their environment. Sommeliers describe the provenance of wine as *terroir*, which speaks to the literal earth and area where the grapes were grown. The same kinds of descriptions can be applied to oysters, and because this form of sea life literally filters the water that it grows in, oysters pick up the taste of the area. Species also defines the flavor. At Hog Island, the oysters are all slightly different:

–**Pacific Sweetwater Oysters** are their signature oyster. They are plump and rich with a smoky-sweet flavor. They have fluted, oval-shaped shells.

–**Atlantic Oysters**, also called Blue Point, are originally from the Atlantic Ocean but grow quite well in the Tomales Bay. They have a smooth, thick shell that is oblong with a green tint. They have a delicate taste that is slightly salty with a mineral finish.

–**Kumamoto Oysters** are originally from Japan. Americans really love Kumamotos, perhaps because they are small and very easy to eat. Lots of people learn to love oysters from eating these sweet, plump oysters with a buttery texture. They have a small, deep-cupped shell, which is why they stay little but get fat.

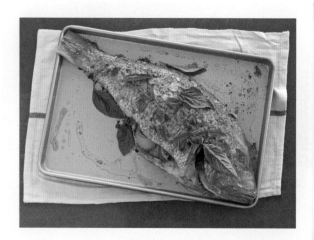

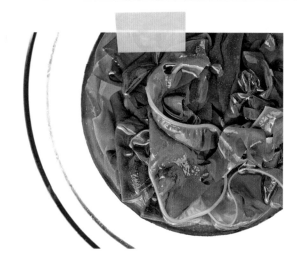

OYSTER SANGRITA   MAKES 4 COCKTAILS

This is sort of an appetizer and cocktail at the same time. The mix of tangy citrus, tomato and spice wakes up the palate and is a great way to start a meal.

½   cup fresh orange juice
¼   cup fresh lime juice
¼   cup fresh lemon juice
½   cup tomato juice
¼   cup kosher salt
2   tablespoons sugar
1   teaspoon chili powder
¼   teaspoon cayenne pepper
½   teaspoon smoked paprika, divided
½   lime
8   oysters, shucked, reserving the liquor
4   ounces tequila

In a medium pitcher, stir together the orange juice, lime juice, lemon juice and tomato juice and refrigerate until cold.

In a shallow dish, mix the kosher salt with the sugar, chili powder, cayenne and ¼ teaspoon of the paprika. Wet the rims of 4 cocktail glasses with the lime. Lightly dip the wet rim in the spiced salt mixture.

Place 2 shucked oysters in each glass, dividing the oyster liquor equally among the glasses. Lightly sprinkle the oysters with a pinch of the remaining paprika.

Pour 1 ounce of tequila into each glass and top with the orange juice mixture. Serve immediately.

OYSTER AND SEA LETTUCE SALAD WITH ANCHOVY VINAIGRETTE   SERVES 4

This recipe was developed after a visit to the oyster beds at Hog Island Oyster Company in Marshall, California. Bright green "sea lettuce," a type of seaweed, was growing on top of the oyster cages. It was delicious, and inspired me to make this salad when we came back to shore.

20   oysters, shucked, reserving the liquor
3   tablespoons fresh lemon juice, strained
3   tablespoons fresh lime juice, strained
3   oil-packed anchovy fillets, minced
6   tablespoons extra virgin olive oil
1   jalapeño pepper, seeded and minced
–   fine sea salt and freshly ground pepper
6   ounces fresh sea lettuce (see note)
2   heads baby bok choy, thinly sliced
1   small red bell pepper, thinly sliced
1   scallion, thinly sliced
½   cup croutons (see note)

Stir the reserved oyster liquor, lemon juice, lime juice and minced anchovies in a bowl. Whisk in the olive oil and add the jalapeño. Season to taste with salt and pepper.

Toss the sea lettuce, baby bok choy, red bell pepper and scallions in a large bowl with enough anchovy vinaigrette to coat. Season to taste with salt and pepper.

Divide the salad equally onto 4 plates. Top with the croutons and oysters and serve immediately.

Note: To make homemade croutons, cut half a loaf of crusty Italian bread into 1-inch cubes, then place the bread cubes in a bowl, drizzle with a generous amount of olive oil and toss to coat. Place the bread cubes in a single layer on a baking sheet and bake until they are crisp and golden brown, about 5 to 8 minutes.

Note: If fresh sea lettuce is not available, use wakame, a salted sea lettuce available at Japanese markets and natural food stores. Rinse and soak the wakame in ice water for at least 1 hour before using.

71

HOG WASH   —*adapted from Hog Island Oyster Company*

This recipe comes from the wonderful people at the Hog Island Oyster Company. It is a type of mignonette with jalapeño and cilantro. The flavor is bright and spicy but still allows the flavor of the oysters to come through.

MAKES ABOUT ½ CUP

⅓   *cup rice wine vinegar*
½   *bunch cilantro, finely chopped*
1   *large shallot, finely diced*
1   *large jalapeño chili, seeded
    and finely diced*
1   *lime, juiced*
2   *tablespoons mirin*
1   *teaspoon sugar*

Mix well and serve with oysters on the half shell.

BALSAMIC MIGNONETTE   MAKES ABOUT ½ CUP

This recipe is a little different than classic mignonette in that there is both balsamic vinegar and sherry vinegar, which cuts the sweetness of the balsamic just a bit.

¼   *cup balsamic vinegar*
2   *tablespoons sherry vinegar*
2   *tablespoons finely minced shallot*
2   *teaspoons freshly cracked black pepper*
–   *water as needed*

Stir the balsamic vinegar, sherry vinegar, shallot and black pepper in a small bowl. Dilute the mignonette with water, as needed, if the vinegar is too strong. Serve with oysters on the half shell.

ROASTED OYSTERS WITH GREMOLATA   SERVES 4

Oysters that have been roasted are more briny. After topping the raw oysters with
a classic mixture of garlic, parsley and lemon zest, the oysters are then nestled into a
pan of salt to cook.

4   *cups kosher salt*
2   *dozen oysters on the half shell*
½   *cup unsalted butter, melted*
3   *tablespoons chopped Italian parsley*
1   *tablespoon grated lemon zest*
1   *garlic clove, minced*
2   *lemons, halved*

Set the oven to broil. Mix 2 cups of the kosher salt in a large bowl with
just enough water to form the consistency of wet sand. Pour the remaining 2 cups of salt on a medium baking sheet. Gently nestle the oysters on
the dry salt to balance them and brush each oyster with butter.

Stir the parsley, lemon zest and garlic in a small bowl to blend. Top each
oyster with a pinch of the gremolata.

Broil the oysters for 3 to 4 minutes, or until the butter is bubbling and
lightly browned.

Finish with a squeeze of fresh lemon juice. Serve the oysters on a bed of
the wet salt.

STEAMED CLAMS IN WHITE WINE-CHORIZO BROTH

Clams are more assertive and briny than oysters. The stronger character holds up very well
when steamed with white wine and spicy chorizo. For this dish, choose smaller clams that
are more tender.

SERVES 4

3   *tablespoons extra virgin olive oil*
¼   *cup thinly sliced Spanish chorizo*
1   *small shallot, thinly sliced*
1   *garlic clove, thinly sliced*
4   *pounds small clams, such as cockles,*
    scrubbed and soaked
1   *teaspoon freshly ground black pepper*
1   *cup dry white wine*
3   *tablespoons unsalted butter*
2   *tablespoons chopped Italian parsley*

Heat the olive oil in a large sauté pan over medium heat. When the oil
is hot, add the chorizo, shallot and garlic and sauté until aromatic, about
3 minutes.

Add the clams, season with black pepper and deglaze with the white
wine. Cover the pan and steam the clams until they open, about 8 to 10
minutes.

Add the butter and parsley and gently toss to combine. Serve the clams
in bowls with fresh bread.

73

MUSSELS WITH TOMATO-SAFFRON BUTTER

Mussels cooked in garlic and white wine is a classic combination, and the saffron threads incorporated into lemon juice and butter give the broth in this dish its beautiful orange-red color.

SERVES 4

1 teaspoon (tightly packed) saffron threads
2 tablespoons fresh lemon juice
4 tablespoons soft unsalted butter
– fine sea salt and freshly ground
   black pepper
4 pounds mussels
3 tablespoons extra virgin olive oil
2 garlic cloves, sliced
½ cup diced seeded peeled tomatoes
½ cup dry white wine
3 tablespoons chopped Italian parsley
– crusty bread

In a small mixing bowl, steep the saffron in the lemon juice for 5 minutes. Add the softened butter and whisk until fully blended. Season to taste with salt and pepper.

Scrub the mussels well under cold running water, discarding any with broken shells. Remove the beards from the mussels.

Heat the olive oil in a heavy large skillet over medium-high heat. Add the garlic and sauté until lightly toasted, about 1 minute. Add the mussels, tomatoes, white wine and parsley; toss to combine. Add the saffron butter, cover the skillet and cook the mussels until they all open, about 3 minutes. Season to taste with salt and pepper. Serve in bowls with crusty bread.

PHYLLO-WRAPPED SALMON WITH LEMON-HORSERADISH CREAM

The crispy flakes of phyllo in this recipe make a nice textural contrast to the tender salmon inside. This technique is an elegant way to serve salmon fillets, and the lemon-horseradish cream adds brightness and a little bit of a kick to the dish.

SERVES 4

8 (3-ounce) salmon fillets,
   skin and pin bones removed
– fine sea salt and freshly ground pepper
4 large basil leaves
4 tablespoons unsalted butter, melted
4 sheets phyllo dough
½ cup sour cream
2 tablespoons prepared horseradish
1 tablespoon fresh lemon juice
½ teaspoon grated lemon zest
1 tablespoon thinly sliced chives
3 tablespoons canola oil

Season the salmon fillets on all sides with salt and pepper. Lay 1 basil leaf on top of 1 salmon fillet, and place another fillet on top to make a sandwich. Repeat with the remaining salmon and basil.

Brush the top of 1 phyllo sheet with melted butter, fold the sheet in half, then brush the top with more butter. Place 1 salmon-basil fillet on 1 end of the phyllo dough and wrap neatly. Repeat with the remaining phyllo, butter and salmon-basil fillets.

Stir the sour cream, horseradish, lemon juice and zest in a bowl to blend. Season the horseradish cream to taste with salt and pepper and stir in the chives.

Divide the canola oil between 2 nonstick sauté pans and heat the oil over medium heat. Add 2 phyllo-wrapped salmon fillets to each pan and cook for about 4 minutes on each side, or until the phyllo is golden brown and a metal skewer can be easily inserted into the salmon. When the skewer is left in the salmon for 5 seconds it will feel just warm when touched to the lip. Serve the salmon fillets with the horseradish cream.

75

WHOLE ROASTED RED SNAPPER
WITH THAI SPICES AND COCONUT RICE   SERVES 4

I really love cooking whole fish, and you can impart lots of great flavor by stuffing the cavity with herbs and lemons. This dish incorporates flavors inspired by the food of Southeast Asia.

RED SNAPPER

- 1 *(4-pound) whole red snapper, head on, scales removed and cleaned*
- – *fine sea salt and freshly ground black pepper*
- ⅓ *cup canola oil*
- 3 *tablespoons unsweetened coconut milk*
- 2 *limes, 1 zested and juiced, 1 cut in half*
- 1 *tablespoon grated ginger*
- 1 *tablespoon ground coriander seeds*
- 1 *garlic clove, sliced*
- ½ *teaspoon chili flakes*
- ¼ *cup basil chiffonade*
- ¼ *cup cilantro chiffonade*

COCONUT RICE

- 1 *cup jasmine rice*
- 1½ *cups water*
- ½ *stalk lemongrass*
- – *fine sea salt and freshly ground white pepper*
- 1 *cup unsweetened coconut milk*
- 1 *tablespoon cilantro chiffonade*
- 1 *lime*

Preheat the oven to 400°F. Generously season inside the belly and both sides of the fish with salt and pepper. Place the fish in a roasting pan.

Combine the canola oil with the coconut milk, lime zest and juice, ginger, coriander, garlic and chili flakes in a bowl and stir to blend. Spoon the spice mixture over the snapper and bake, basting frequently, for 25 to 30 minutes, or until a metal skewer can easily be inserted into the fish and, when left in for 5 seconds, feels warm.

Meanwhile, prepare the rice. Place the rice in a fine-mesh sieve and rinse under cool water until the water begins to run clear. Transfer the rice to a medium pot and add 1n cups of water, lemongrass and a pinch of salt. Bring to a boil over medium-high heat, then lower the heat and simmer for 10 minutes. Remove the rice from the heat, cover and let sit for another 10 minutes. When the rice is cooked, remove and discard the lemongrass. Gently stir in the coconut milk and cilantro and season to taste with lime juice, salt and pepper. Make sure the rice is creamy.

Spoon the coconut rice into the middle of 4 plates. Fillet the snapper, running a knife lengthwise down the fish at about the center to separate the side into 2 fillets, and then under the flesh to separate the fillets from the bones. Carefully lift off each fillet and place it on top of the rice. When the top fillets have been removed, lift off the fish bones and portion the bottom fillets in the same manner. Plate the remaining fillets and spoon some of the sauce from the roasting pan over each portion. Finish each dish with a squeeze of fresh lime juice and garnish with the chiffonade of basil and cilantro.

WINE PAIRINGS

In Southeast Asia, flavors like rich coconut milk, lemongrass, cilantro, basil and spicy chili flakes are standard ingredients. These flavors go very well with seafood and we love using them, but it can be challenging to pair wine with dishes that are so robust. The two wines featured here are quite different from each other but each compliments the snapper wonderfully.

THE JOHANN'S GARDEN 2008. Henschke Barossa, Australia

This lovely wine is made up of 68% Grenache, 17% Mourvèdre and 15% Shiraz grapes from selected vineyards growing in the Barossa region of Australia (Barossa Valley and Eden Valley). The Grenache, Mourvèdre and Shiraz are vinified separately and matured in older French hogheads for 12 months prior to blending and bottling. The Johann's Garden is a fairly powerful wine, with a rich and smoky fruit, soft silky tannins and quite a long finish. Initially it might not make sense to choose such a rich wine with the snapper, but you'll see that the softness of the wine brings harmony into the seasoning of the snapper and combines with the creaminess of the coconut rice.

DR. LOOSEN BLUE SLATE ESTATE KABINETT RIESLING 2007.
Mosel-Saar-Ruwer, Germany

Riesling is, without a doubt, one of the greatest grape varieties and is often undervalued because people fear the fruitiness and the residual sugar, but sometimes a little fruitiness can be very useful in pairings because it rounds it up. Rieslings are especially good paired with Thai cuisine because they show their strong side, which helps to balance the delicate, spicy and rich flavors.

The Dr. Loosen Estate has been in the same family for over 200 years. When Ernst Loosen assumed ownership in 1988, he realized that with ungrafted vines averaging 60 years old in some of Germany's best-rated vineyards, he had the raw materials to create stunningly intense, world-class wines. Ernst dramatically reduced his crop size and stopped all chemical fertilization, allowing only moderate use of organic fertilizers. Most important, he turned to gentler cellar practices that allow the wine to develop to its full potential with a minimum of handling and technological meddling.

SEAWEED AND HERB SALAD
WITH TOASTED SESAME SEEDS AND PONZU VINAIGRETTE

This recipe incorporates wakame, a type of seaweed, with some traditional Japanese flavors. Yuzu, a citrus fruit resembling a small grapefruit, is used in the vinaigrette and shiso leaves, a strong leafy herb from the mint family, are mixed with the greens.

SERVES 4

PONZU VINAIGRETTE

- 3 *tablespoons rice wine vinegar*
- 2 *tablespoons fresh lime juice*
- 2 *tablespoons mirin*
- 2 *tablespoons soy sauce*
- 2 *tablespoons yuzu juice*
- – *fine sea salt and freshly ground pepper*
- ¼ *cup olive oil*
- ¼ *cup canola oil*

SALAD

- 6 *ounces salted wakame, rinsed and soaked for at least 1 hour*
- 1 *cup mixed baby lettuces*
- ¼ *cup fresh mint leaves, torn*
- 3-4 *fresh shiso leaves, torn*
- 1 *tablespoon toasted sesame seeds*

Whisk the rice wine vinegar, lime juice, mirin, soy sauce and yuzu in a large bowl to blend. Season to taste with salt and pepper. Whisking constantly, slowly drizzle in the canola oil and olive oil. The vinaigrette can be made up to 2 days ahead and stored in the refrigerator. Rewhisk the vinaigrette before using.

Drain the wakame and blot it dry to remove any excess water. Cut the wakame into thin matchstick-size strips (julienne). Gently combine the wakame, baby lettuces, mint and shiso leaves in another large bowl.

Sprinkle the toasted sesame seeds over the salad and toss the salad with enough of the ponzu vinaigrette to evenly coat it; season to taste with salt and pepper and gently toss the salad again to coat. Serve immediately.

SPICED HOT CHOCOLATE AND CINNAMON BEIGNETS

Beignets are a doughnut-like pastry most famous, perhaps, in New Orleans, Louisiana. A tasty dough is deep fried and puffed into little pillows that are then sprinkled with sugar and cinnamon. They're perfect for dipping into hot chocolate.

SERVES 4

BEIGNETS

- 3 cups canola oil
- ¼ cup sugar
- ¼ teaspoon ground cinnamon
- ½ cup unsalted butter
- ½ cup water
- ½ cup whole milk
- ¼ teaspoon fine salt
- 1 cup all-purpose flour
- 3 whole eggs

HOT CHOCOLATE

- ¼ cup skinned toasted hazelnuts
- 1 vanilla bean, cut into 1-inch pieces
- 1 tablespoon grated panela (piloncillo; see note)
- 1 tablespoon sugar
- – zest of 1 orange
- 2 cups whole milk
- ½ cup heavy cream
- 1 cinnamon stick
- 1 star anise
- 1 2-inch chile de arbol
- 3 ounces dark chocolate
- – pinch fine sea salt

Heat the oil in a wide, shallow pot over medium-low heat until it reaches 375°F on a deep-fry thermometer. While the oil is heating, combine the sugar and cinnamon in a bowl and reserve.

Bring the butter, water, milk and salt to a boil in a saucepan over medium-high heat. Using a silicone spatula, stir in the flour, then reduce the heat to low and stir continuously until the mixture begins to pull away from the sides of the pan and forms a ball, 1 to 2 minutes. Remove the saucepan from the heat. Add the eggs, one at a time, and stir to blend well after each addition. Transfer the mixture to a piping bag fitted with a large plain tip.

Using scissors to cut the dough, carefully drop 1-inch-long strips of dough into the hot oil. Fry until golden brown, turning once, about 2 minutes on each side. Drain on paper towels, then roll the beignets in the sugar and cinnamon mixture.

Combine the hazelnuts, vanilla bean pieces, panela, sugar and orange zest in a food processor and grind to a coarse consistency.

In a medium saucepan, combine the hazelnut mixture with the milk, cream, cinnamon, star anise and chile de arbol and bring to a boil. Reduce the heat to low and simmer for 10 minutes. Whisk in the chocolate and salt, stirring until melted. Simmer for another 10 minutes, then strain through a fine-mesh sieve and serve immediately with the warm beignets.

Note: Panela, also known as piloncillo, is an unrefined palm sugar used in Latin America; it is available at Latin markets and specialty markets. If it is unavailable, light brown sugar can be used instead.

Chapter 4

BIRTH OF A DISH

Livorno, Italy

LIVORNO, ITALY.

A RECIPE, BY DEFINITION, IS A SET OF INSTRUCTIONS REQUIRED TO PREPARE A PARTICULAR DISH, AS WELL AS A LIST OF THE INGREDIENTS REQUIRED TO GET TO THE END RESULT. BUT WHO WRITES THAT RECIPE? It could be a great chef, a food scientist, a home economist, a food writer or a good home cook. New recipes get written all the time from simply tweaking the standard form of a classic formula. Some cooks are fearless and will just start throwing things into the mix, and some people are terrified to do anything different. Both approaches are not really good because you are either paralyzed by fear and no creativity comes out, or you might hit on something perfect once but because there was no documentation or real process to the execution, it gets lost. Some recipes are written out of necessity, dictated by a lack of certain ingredients, or out of an excess of ingredients. Without inspiration, even the most basic recipe ends up being just a formula with no soul. For me, it's important to have a point of reference, either from a dish that I have enjoyed in the past, a place that I have visited, or many times both.

A recent visit to Livorno, a coastal town in the Tuscan region of Italy, was a little like stepping back in time. It is a bustling city, but the architecture is old and beautiful, and you can just tell that the area is full of tradition. A huge, open-air farmers' market is set up there every week, and walking through the market wakes up all of your senses. The smell of fresh fruits and vegetables, cheese and coffee and the sounds of vendors calling out to potential customers fill the air. The stalls are packed with all kinds of fresh vegetables. When I was there, porcini mushrooms had just come into season, and the farmers had put together impressive displays of the huge mushrooms. There were all kinds of greens and squash, fresh fava beans and radicchio. One vendor sold all different kinds of nuts and *pignoli* (pine nuts). There was beautiful citrus fruit from Sardinia and grapes from all around Italy. Livorno is a large port city and boats loaded down with products from all over Europe come into its harbor.

The harbor in Livorno is very busy. The fishermen who gather there every day have just come in from working at sea, are just getting ready to go out to sea, or are retired and now just come there to hang out with their friends or to work the fish market that is located right on the docks. One morning, when I went to see what the fishermen were bringing in and selling that day, I had the opportunity to visit with them. They had an impressive variety of fish and sea creatures, including octopi and squid. It was great to hear them talk about the many years they had been fishing and working on boats. Most of them had been all over the world by boat, stopping in exotic ports and experiencing the different cultures. Fishing is difficult work but has offered these men an adventurous life.

83

A chef from the Hotel Gran Duca, which is a classic Livorno hotel that sits right on the shore, showed us his version of *cacciucco*—the fisherman's stew that is famous in Livorno (*recipe p. 96*). The recipe is based on a hearty fish stew that the fishermen would make for themselves from either the fish that didn't sell that day at the market or the lesser-known fish that got caught in the nets and are more difficult to sell. The origins of the recipe are based on just the simple ingredients that the fishermen would have—fish (always incredibly fresh, of course), some red wine, garlic, and even perhaps some stale bread to use in the stew. It was not something that the fishermen or cooks felt was a humble dish. In fact, it would have been a favorite recipe—sort of like coastal Italian comfort food. The recipe is about using all of the ingredients and not wasting anything. Today, with a nod to the old recipe, the dish usually contains cuttlefish, octopus, squid and various shellfish, as well as finfish—depending on what is brought in that day. The fish are cooked in a red wine and tomato-based sauce and poured over bread that has been flavored with garlic. Restaurants and hotels up and down this part of the coast picked up the dish, perhaps refined it just a little, and now serve it to pay homage to the tradition and to the fishermen themselves.

Sometimes humble, honest food can be the most inspiring. The birth of a dish starts with a story—either of the people who work with ingredients or of a very basic recipe. Usually it has to do with the products that come from a certain place or with a traditional technique of that place. I was very inspired by the cacciucco I tasted in Livorno and was anxious to go back to Le Bernardin to create a dish that uses a seafood, tomato, and red wine sauce—like the cacciucco sauce—as the base. I wasn't sure when or how the recipe would happen, but I knew I wanted to draw upon the story and the flavor to help me create something new.

When I, or one of the other chefs, have an inspiration for a dish, we usually get together to brainstorm before we prepare the dish in a couple of different ways and do some trial tasting. The inspiration for this new dish comes from a humble fisherman's stew, but the dishes at Le Bernardin must be very refined, so it can be a bit of a challenge to rework it into a sophisticated recipe. All of the chefs agree that cod will be a great main focus to our new dish. Fresh-caught cod is a delicious, light, flaky fish that has enough body to stand up to heavier sauces and elevates the humble nature of traditional cacciucco to a refined level. Using octopus meat and squid ink along with the red wine will bring an earthy quality to the sauce and will be a great translation of the cacciucco flavors. We all agree

PREPARING the CACCIUCCO.

CEPHALOPODS

85

Octopus, squid and cuttlefish are all in a class of mollusks that are quite biologically advanced. They all share two characteristics—tentacles and ink sacs that they use as a "shield" against predators. These creatures can add great flavor and texture to a recipe. When purchasing, buy fresh product that smells of the ocean—fresh and salty—but never fishy. Always follow a particular recipe's cooking instructions but remember that generally these creatures either need to be flash-cooked over very high heat or cooked for a long time on lower heat. Anything in between will result in a very rubbery texture.

that the dish needs color and some spice, so the idea of either using a hot pepper oil or making a pepper sauce into a foam (a technique for changing the texture of a traditional sauce into something very light and airy) will bring color and heat to the dish. The fish is topped with a little bit of a fresh pepper salad, consisting of very thin strips of mixed peppers tossed in a little fresh lemon juice. The pepper salad adds acidity but also looks beautiful on the fish. Each of the elements tastes really good alone, but we must make sure they work together. As we do a tasting, we assemble the dish and realize that we need to make a couple of modifications, like eliminate some lime zest from the pepper salad, and decide whether the foam or oil tastes better with the entire dish. Overall, we agree that it is a good effort and worthy of serving to the guests, first as a special; as we get some feedback, we can see if it will work on the main menu.

Creating a new dish and writing recipes could very well be the greatest challenge for a chef, but it is very satisfying to see an inspiration turn into something special that ends up on our menu. Memory plays an important part in how I cook, and sometimes, while traveling, I'm both inspired by what I experience and reminded of things that I have seen and enjoyed in the past. Being in Livorno—walking through the market and being so close to the sea—reminded me of my childhood years in Antibes, France. The smells and sounds were very familiar. The cacciucco and red wine sauce made me think of the fish dishes that are prepared in the Basque region of Europe—a region where I lived as a teenager. It is so interesting how sights, smells and tastes revive memories.

After my visit to Italy and the experience of making the new dish at Le Bernardin, I really wanted to make a dish at home that had some of the same ingredients as the cacciucco and the dish we invented at the restaurant. In the same spirit of using a tomato and red wine sauce, I made a *Basquaise* sauce, which is a classic sauce from the Basque country. It involves cooking tomatoes and peppers together until they are very soft. I put a little twist on it by using red wine in the sauce to remind me of the similar sauce in the cacciucco. Served with seared cod, it really reminded me of both my childhood and my recent trip to Livorno. Even though I'm a chef, I still enjoy simple, pared-down dishes, especially at home. It's important to me to share my experiences and background with my young son and, many times, food helps me do that.

COD BASQUAISE SERVES 4

Cod is a delicious, sturdy, white-fleshed fish. So many people only know salted cod, but codfish is very versatile and can stand up to hearty sauces and strong cooking techniques. Inspired by the cacciucco I ate in Italy and my memory of the sauces of the Basque country, where I spent some time as a child, I developed this dish using a sauce with a tomato and red wine base.

BASQUAISE

- 3   *tablespoons olive oil*
- ½   *cup finely diced yellow onion*
- 1   *teaspoon minced garlic*
- ¼   *cup small diced serrano ham*
- ½   *cup small diced red bell pepper*
- ½   *cup small diced yellow bell pepper*
- 1   *cup diced seeded peeled tomato*
- 1   *teaspoon chopped fresh thyme leaves*
- ½   *cup dry red wine*
- 1   *tablespoon chopped fresh*
     Italian parsley
- –   *fine sea salt and freshly ground*
     white pepper
- –   *piment d'Espelette*

COD

- 2   *tablespoons canola oil*
- 4   *(6-ounce) cod fillets*
- –   *fine sea salt and freshly ground*
     white pepper
- 2   *thyme sprigs*
- 2   *garlic cloves, peeled and halved*

Heat the olive oil in a heavy large sauté pan over medium-low heat. Add the onion and sauté until tender, about 5 minutes. Add the garlic and continue cooking until tender, about 2 minutes. Add the ham and bell peppers and sauté until the peppers are soft, about 5 minutes. Reduce the heat to low. Add the diced tomato and thyme and simmer, stirring often, until slightly thickened, about 20 minutes. Add the red wine and cook out the alcohol, about 10 to 15 minutes. Stir in the chopped parsley and season to taste with salt, white pepper and piment d'Espelette. This Basquaise can be made 1 day ahead; cool, then cover and refrigerate.

Heat a griddle or a griddle pan over medium-high heat until it is very hot, then add the canola oil. Season the cod on both sides with salt and pepper. Add the cod to the pan along with the thyme and garlic. Lower the heat to medium and cook until the fish is golden brown on the bottom, 6 to 8 minutes. Turn the fish over and finish cooking until a metal skewer can be easily inserted into the fish and, when left in the fish for 5 seconds, feels just warm when touched to the lip, another 2 to 3 minutes.

Meanwhile, heat the Basquaise until hot. Spoon the Basquaise onto plates, place the cod in the center and serve immediately.

WINE PAIRINGS

A classic Basquaise (from the Basque region of Europe) sauce is made with red wine and a combination of peppers resulting in a very distinct flavor. Two very different wines have been chosen to pair with this recipe—Bordeaux as well as a Pinot Noir. Like the recipe, both of these selections have some complexity to their history as well as their flavor profiles.

CHÂTEAU HAUT-BERGEY, PESSAC-LÉOGNAN 2005. Bordeaux, France

Chateau Haut Bergey is located just south of Bordeaux in the town of Léognan. The size of the vineyard is 56 acres – 60 % planted in Cabernet Sauvignon and the rest in Merlot and the vines are 30 years old, which contributes to more complexity. The wine is very clean a pure in the fruit and the Cabernet Sauvignon delivers its typical firm Tannins that make Bordeaux so special. The exceptional Vintage 2005 is thought, by many wine critics to be the vintage of the century.

PAUL CLUVER PINOT NOIR 2008. Elgin Valley, South Africa

For the past few years wine makers seem to be very focused on growing grapes in so called "cool climate areas" where Chardonnay and Pinot Noir find ideal conditions. One of these areas is Elgin, South Africa. In a blind tasting, these wines can be tricky to identify because they have characteristics from the old and new world. That means that these wines have a very generous fruit (new world), medium in alcohol (old world), soft acidity (new world) and slightly firm tannins (old world). Paul Cluver is a family-run winery and their Pinot Noir is oriented on red Burgundy. It possesses fairly complex fruit with a beautiful earthiness and also shows some minerality which is quite unusual for a new world Pinot.

CHARRED OCTOPUS WITH PEACH, ARUGULA AND AGED BALSAMIC

Learning to cook octopus properly is important because it can become a bit rubbery if not prepared correctly. This recipe teaches a great technique. The richness of the aged balsamic vinegar, the brightness of the peach, and the peppery bite of arugula come together in a harmonious way that celebrates all of the flavors, especially the octopus.

SERVES 4

½ *small onion, peeled and quartered*
1 *small celery stalk, sliced on the bias*
½ *small carrot, peeled and sliced on the bias*
1 *3–ounce piece prosciutto*
2 *fresh Italian parsley sprigs*
3 *garlic cloves, cut in half*
½ *teaspoon cayenne pepper*
8 *cups water, approx.*
2 *pounds octopus, head removed and tentacles separated*
2 *tablespoons olive oil*
– *fine sea salt and freshly ground black pepper*
½ *cup baby arugula*
1 *peach, halved, pitted, and thinly sliced*
4 *tablespoons aged (at least 8 years) balsamic vinegar*
1 *lemon, cut in half*

Combine the onion, celery, carrot, prosciutto, parsley, garlic and cayenne pepper in a pot with about 8 cups of water. Season the water with salt and boil for 5 minutes to allow the flavors to infuse. Add the octopus and reduce the heat to medium-low. Simmer gently for about 1 hour or until the octopus is tender when gently pierced with a knife. Cool the octopus in the braising liquid at room temperature until cool enough to handle.

Remove the octopus from the braising liquid and drain well. Heat a cast-iron skillet or a flat griddle over high heat until it is very hot. Season the octopus with olive oil, salt and pepper. Grill the octopus until it is caramelized and crusted on all sides, about 3 to 5 minutes. Transfer the charred octopus to a cutting board and cut each tentacle on the bias into 4 slices.

Place the octopus slices in the center of 4 plates and garnish with arugula and 3 to 4 slices of the peach. Drizzle 1 tablespoon of aged balsamic vinegar over and around the octopus, and finish each dish with a squeeze of lemon juice. Serve immediately.

BAKED ZUCCHINI WITH SEASONED BREAD CRUMBS

Zucchini is one of those vegetables that always seems to be in abundance. This dish is so easy to make quickly and it is a great way to use all of those extra squash from the garden.

SERVES 4

½ *cup olive oil*
½ *cup basil leaves*
½ *cup Italian parsley leaves*
2 *tablespoons fresh oregano leaves*
1 *garlic clove, thinly sliced*
½ *cup dried bread crumbs*
¼ *cup water*
– *fine sea salt and freshly ground black pepper*
4 *small zucchini, cut in half lengthwise*

93

Preheat the oven to 400°F. Combine the olive oil, basil, parsley, oregano and garlic in a food processor and blend well. Add the bread crumbs and water and blend to create a smooth paste. Season to taste with salt and pepper.

Arrange the zucchini halves in a 12x9-inch gratin dish. Season the zucchini with salt and pepper, and spread a thin layer of the bread crumb mixture over the zucchini. Bake until the zucchini are tender and the crust is golden brown, 10 to 12 minutes.

GRILLED CALAMARI WITH QUINOA, TOMATOES AND OLIVES

This salad utilizes quinoa, which is a fairly quick-cooking grain with a nice, nutty flavor. Inspired by the flavors of the Mediterranean, the quinoa is tossed with parsley, mint, tomatoes, olives and lemon, then topped with the grilled calamari. Grilling the calamari brings out its rich, earthy flavor.

SERVES 4

- 1 cup quinoa
- 2 plum tomatoes, seeded and diced
- ¼ cup extra virgin olive oil, plus more for brushing and drizzling
- ¼ cup sliced green olives
- 3 tablespoons fresh lemon juice
- 2 tablespoons chopped fresh Italian parsley
- 2 tablespoons fresh mint, julienned
- – fine sea salt and freshly ground black pepper
- 6 ounces calamari tubes

Place the quinoa in a fine-mesh sieve and rinse under cold water for 3 to 4 minutes; drain well. Bring 2 cups of water to a boil in a heavy saucepan over high heat and stir in the quinoa. Reduce the heat to medium-low and simmer gently, uncovered, until the quinoa is tender, 10 to 12 minutes. Remove the pan from the heat, cover, and let stand for 10 minutes. Drain off the excess water and let cool.

Mix the quinoa in a bowl with the tomatoes, ¼ cup of the olive oil, olives, lemon juice, parsley and mint. Season to taste with salt and pepper.

Preheat the grill over high heat. Season the calamari tubes with salt and pepper and brush them with olive oil. Grill the calamari until they are just opaque, turning once, about 5 minutes. Transfer the cooked calamari to a cutting board and slice the tubes crosswise into rings.

Spoon the quinoa salad onto the center of 4 plates. Top with the grilled calamari, drizzle some olive oil around, and serve immediately.

FENNEL POLLEN-DUSTED WHOLE BRANZINO WITH WHITE WINE, TOMATOES AND FENNEL BROTH

During my travels throughout northern California and Tuscany, I saw lots of wild fennel growing on the side of the road. Many people know how to use fennel bulbs, fronds and seeds, but the pollen of the fennel has a distinct flavor and a beautiful yellow color. It is available online and in specialty stores, but it is also fun to collect your own from the wild plants on the side of the road.

SERVES 4

- 4 whole branzino (about 1 pound each), scales removed and cleaned
- – fine sea salt and freshly ground black pepper
- 1 tablespoon fennel pollen
- 4 tablespoons extra virgin olive oil
- 2 shallots, thinly sliced
- 3 garlic cloves, thinly sliced
- 1 fennel bulb, cored and sliced
- ½ cup dry white wine
- ¼ cup water
- 1 pint cherry tomatoes
- ¼ cup julienned fresh Italian parsley
- 2 tablespoons butter
- ¼ teaspoon dried hot red chili flakes

Preheat the oven to 425°F.

Generously season inside the belly and both sides of each of the fish with salt and pepper. Place the fish on a roasting pan and lightly dust both sides with fennel pollen. Drizzle 2 tablespoons of the olive oil over the fish.

Heat the remaining 2 tablespoons of olive oil in a large skillet over medium heat. Add the shallots and garlic and sauté until they start to caramelize, about 7 minutes. Add the sliced fennel, white wine, and ¼ cup of water and bring the mixture to a simmer. Add the cherry tomatoes, parsley, butter and chili flakes. Season the broth with salt and pepper. Remove the pan from the heat and pour the sauce into the roasting pan with the fish. Bake the fish until a metal skewer can easily be inserted and, when left in for 5 seconds, feels warm on the lower lip, 12 to 15 minutes.

Transfer each fish to a plate and spoon the vegetables and broth over the fish. Serve immediately.

PAN ROASTED COD WITH OCTOPUS–RED WINE SAUCE
AND BASQUAISE EMULSION —*adapted from Le Bernardin*

Fishermen's stews are traditional and popular in coastal towns all over the world. They're usually a mixture of lots of different kinds of fish and many times include octopus and squid. Octopus definitely gives an earthy flavor to a dish, and as this recipe was being developed, it was obvious that we needed a bit of an earthy base to round out the flavor of the entire recipe. The octopus was the perfect solution.

SERVES 4

OCTOPUS-RED WINE SAUCE

- 2 *tablespoons canola oil*
- 8 *ounces octopus, rinsed and cut into 1-inch pieces*
- 2 *garlic cloves, sliced*
- 2 *tablespoons tomato paste*
- 1 *cup dry red wine*
- 1 *cup mushroom stock, reduced to ⅔ cup (recipe p. 29)*
- – *fine sea salt and freshly ground white pepper*

BASQUAISE EMULSION

- ¼ *cup olive oil*
- ½ *cup diced yellow onion*
- ½ *cup diced red bell pepper*
- ½ *cup diced yellow bell pepper*
- 1 *tablespoon minced garlic*
- 1 *cup diced tomato*
- 1 *slice prosciutto*
- – *fine sea salt and freshly ground black pepper*
- – *piment d'Espelette*
- ¼ *cup water*

COD

- 4 *tablespoons canola oil*
- 4 *(6-ounce) cod fillets*
- – *fine sea salt and freshly ground white pepper*
- – *Wondra flour for dusting*
- 1 *small red bell pepper, sliced into thin rings*
- 1 *small yellow bell pepper, sliced into thin rings*
- 1 *small banana pepper, sliced into thin rings*
- ½ *lemon*
- 2 *tablespoons olive oil*

For the octopus-red wine sauce: Heat the canola oil in a heavy saucepan over high heat until it is very hot. Carefully add the octopus and sear quickly on all sides, about 4 minutes. When the pieces are seared, drain off half of the liquid released by the octopus and lower the heat to medium. Add the garlic and cook until soft. Add the tomato paste and continue cooking for about 3 minutes, stirring frequently to prevent scorching, then pour the red wine into the pan and simmer until reduced to ¼ cup. Add the mushroom stock and bring the sauce to a boil. Lower the heat and simmer for about 20 minutes or until the sauce has reduced slightly and thickened. Season the sauce to taste with salt and pepper. Strain the sauce and set aside until ready to use.

For the Basquaise emulsion: Heat the olive oil in a heavy sauté pan over medium-low heat. Add the onion and sauté until tender, about 5 minutes. Add the bell peppers and garlic and continue cooking until the peppers are soft, about 5 minutes. Add the tomato and prosciutto and cook over low heat, stirring often, for 20 to 30 minutes, or until slightly thickened. Season to taste with salt, pepper and piment d'Espelette. Place the Basquaise in a blender jar and puree, slowly adding the water, until smooth.

For the cod: Divide the canola oil between 2 ovenproof sauté pans and heat over medium-high heat until the oil is very hot but not smoking. Season the cod on both sides with salt and pepper and lightly dust one side with flour. Place the cod in the pan, floured sides down, and sear until golden brown, about 3 minutes. Turn the fish over, put the pans in the oven, and finish cooking the fish in the oven for another 2 to 3 minutes or until a metal skewer can be easily inserted into the fish and, when left in for 5 seconds, feels just warm when touched to the lip. While the cod is cooking, reheat the sauce and the Basquaise, if necessary.

Combine the pepper rings in a bowl; squeeze the lemon over the pepper rings and drizzle them with the olive oil. Season the pepper salad to taste with salt and pepper and toss to coat. Place 1 cod fillet in the center of each of 4 plates. Garnish the top of each fillet with some of the pepper salad. Spoon the octopus-red wine sauce around the plate and spoon a little Basquaise emulsion around the fish. Serve immediately.

CACCIUCCO ALLA LIVORNESE

This historic fishermen's stew comes from Livorno, a coastal town in the Tuscan region of Italy. The use of tomato and red wine creates a bold, flavorful sauce that brings together the mixture of seafood in a hearty, comforting dish.

SERVES 6 TO 8

½ *cup olive oil*
1 *onion, finely diced*
4 *garlic cloves, thinly sliced*
1 *whole octopus (about 6 pounds), head removed, tentacles cut into 1-inch pieces*
1 *cup dry red wine*
1 *tablespoon tomato paste*
4 *cups crushed canned tomatoes*
1 *teaspoon dried hot chili flakes*
½ *pound large shrimp or crayfish, peeled and deveined*
1 *pound mussels, scrubbed and debearded*
1 *pound white-fleshed fish (such as halibut, striped bass or monkfish), cut into 2-inch pieces*
½ *pound calamari, body cut into rings and tentacles cut into 1½- to 2-inch pieces*
6 *thick slices crusty white bread*
1 *garlic clove, peeled*
– *fine sea salt and freshly ground black pepper*
– *extra virgin olive oil*
¼ *cup chopped fresh Italian parsley*

Heat the ½ cup of olive oil in a large sauté pan over medium heat. Add the onion and 4 sliced garlic cloves and sauté until soft and aromatic, about 3 minutes. Add the octopus and cook until opaque, about 10 minutes. Add the red wine and the tomato paste and simmer for another 5 minutes.

Add the crushed tomatoes and chili flakes, then lower the heat and cover the pan. Simmer gently, stirring occasionally, until the octopus is tender, 30 to 40 minutes.

Add the shrimp and cook for 3 minutes, then add the mussels, fish and calamari and cook until the mussels have all opened, about 5 minutes.

Meanwhile, toast the bread slices and rub the toasts with the peeled garlic clove.

Season the stew to taste with salt and pepper. Serve the stew in bowls with extra virgin olive oil and chopped parsley along with the garlic toasts.

BOUILLABAISSE SERVES 4

A mixture of fish and shellfish and a base of tomato and white wine, bouillabaisse is a classic stew from Provence. Much like cacciucco from Italy, this dish has humble beginnings but has been elevated to a national favorite in France. These types of stews honor the idea of using what is available and not wasting anything.

SACHET

3 *Italian parsley sprigs*
2 *thyme sprigs*
1 *bay leaf*
1½ *teaspoons cracked black peppercorns*

BOUILLABAISSE

4 *tablespoons olive oil*
2 *pounds fish bones and parts from firm white-fleshed fish such as halibut or monkfish*
2 *tablespoons tomato paste*
½ *cup Pernod*
1 *onion, diced*
1 *celery stalk, diced*
1 *small fennel bulb, diced*
3 *garlic cloves, sliced*
1 *cup diced tomato*
½ *cup dry white wine*
– *large pinch of saffron threads*
– *fine sea salt and freshly ground white pepper*
12 *small new potatoes, peeled and cut in half*
1 *small leek, tender green parts only, cut into ¼-inch dice*
½ *cup diced fennel, ¼-inch dice*
½ *cup diced onion, ¼-inch dice*
½ *pound firm white fish fillet such as monkfish or halibut, cut into 2-inch chunks*
½ *pound large shrimp, peeled and deveined*
1 *pound mussels and/or clams, scrubbed and soaked (mussels debearded)*
– *country white bread, sliced and toasted*
– *rouille (recipe follows)*

Wrap the parsley, thyme, bay leaf and peppercorns in a sheet of cheesecloth and tie with kitchen twine to enclose. Set aside.

Heat the olive oil in a large pot over medium-high heat. Add the fish bones and heads and sauté about 5 minutes. Add the tomato paste and stir for about 2 minutes. Deglaze with the Pernod and add the diced onion, celery, fennel and garlic. Cook until the vegetables are very soft, stirring often, about 10 minutes. Add the diced tomato, wine and saffron, then add just enough water (about 5 cups) to cover the ingredients. Add the sachet to the soup and simmer 25 to 30 minutes. Season to taste with salt and pepper. Remove the sachet.

Using a hand-held immersion blender, puree the soup in the pot. Strain the soup through a fine-mesh sieve set over a medium pot.

Place the soup over medium heat and add the potatoes, leek, fennel and onion. Simmer until tender, about 15 minutes. Add the clams to the soup and simmer for another 5 minutes. Season the fish with salt and pepper and add it to the bouillabaisse; cook for about 2 minutes. Season the shrimp with salt and pepper and add it, along with the mussels, to the bouillabaisse. Cook until the fish is just barely cooked through and the clams and mussels have opened, about 5 minutes.

Ladle the bouillabaisse into bowls and serve it with toasted country bread and rouille.

ROUILLE
MAKES ¾ CUP

2 *tablespoons water*
1 *teaspoon saffron threads*
2 *large egg yolks*
3 *tablespoons fresh lemon juice*
2 *garlic cloves, very finely minced*
– *fine sea salt and freshly ground white pepper*
6 *tablespoons canola oil*
6 *tablespoons extra virgin olive oil*
– *pinch of cayenne pepper*

Combine the water and saffron in a small bowl and let stand until the saffron threads are moist and the water is very yellow, about 5 minutes.

Combine the saffron mixture, egg yolks, lemon juice and garlic in a blender. Lightly season with salt and pepper and blend on medium speed for about 30 seconds. With the machine running, slowly drizzle in the canola oil and olive oil, being sure the sauce comes together as a thick emulsion and does not break. Blend in the cayenne pepper. Transfer to a tightly sealed container and refrigerate for up to 1 week.

ROASTED STRIPED BASS WITH TOMATOES, ZUCCHINI AND ONIONS

This is an easy dish to prepare and a perfect way to highlight summer vegetables. Roasting the fish and the vegetables together marries their flavors, and the vegetables help keep the top of the fish from cooking too fast and drying out in the oven.

SERVES 4

- 6 tablespoons extra virgin olive oil plus more for coating the parchment
- 1 small onion, quartered, then cut into ⅛-inch slices
- 1 3-pound striped bass fillet
- – fine sea salt and freshly ground white pepper
- 2 teaspoons chopped fresh thyme leaves
- 2 plum tomatoes, halved lengthwise, then cut crosswise into ⅛-inch-thick slices
- 1 small zucchini, halved lengthwise, then cut crosswise into ⅛-inch-thick slices
- 3-4 medium button mushrooms, trimmed and cut into ⅛-inch-thick slices
- 1 lemon, halved
- 2 tablespoons chopped fresh Italian parsley

Preheat the oven to 400°F. Trim a sheet of parchment paper to fit a baking sheet and brush the paper with olive oil.

Heat 3 tablespoons of the olive oil in a sauté pan over medium heat. Add the onion and sauté until soft but not colored.

Season the striped bass with salt and pepper and place it on the prepared baking sheet. Sprinkle the fish with thyme and spread the sautéed onions over the fillet. Make alternating rows of tomato, zucchini, and mushroom slices across the fillet until the fish is completely covered. Drizzle the remaining 3 tablespoons of olive oil over the vegetables and season with salt and pepper.

Roast the fish in the oven for 15 to 20 minutes, occasionally spooning the oil that accumulates on the baking sheet over the fish and vegetables. Halfway through cooking, rotate the baking sheet in the oven. To test for doneness, insert a metal skewer into the center of the fish and hold it there for 5 seconds. The fish is done when the skewer goes in easily and then feels hot when touched to your lip.

Baste the fillet one last time with the oil on the baking sheet and squeeze the juice of the lemon over the fillet. Sprinkle the parsley on top and transfer the fish to a serving platter. Serve immediately.

OLIVE OIL FINANCIER

A *financier* is a little, classic French teacake traditionally made with butter, egg whites and almond flour. This recipe incorporates olive oil, which gives these little cakes a unique flavor and a very nice texture.

MAKES ABOUT 2 DOZEN MINI CAKES

- 6   *tablespoons unsalted butter*
- 1¾ *cups confectioners' sugar*
- ½   *cup almond flour*
- ½   *cup all purpose flour*
- 4   *large egg whites*
- 2   *tablespoons extra virgin olive oil*
- –   *nonstick cooking spray*

Special Equipment
- –   *24 mini muffin (½ ounce) pan*

Cook the butter in a heavy saucepan over medium heat until it is light brown, whisking occasionally, about 6 to 8 minutes. Set the brown butter aside and keep warm. Meanwhile, combine the confectioners' sugar, almond flour and all purpose flour in a medium bowl.

Whisk the egg whites in a large bowl just until frothy and the yellow color dissipates, 1 to 2 minutes. Whisk in the almond flour mixture. Slowly whisk in the warm brown butter, followed by the olive oil, mixing until completely emulsified. Cover and refrigerate for 1 hour.

Meanwhile, preheat the oven to 350°F. Spray the cavities of the muffin pans with nonstick spray and spoon about 1 tablespoon of batter into each cavity. Bake until the cakes are golden brown, 7 to 10 minutes.

Chapter 5

TEAMWORK

Sonoma County, California

102

TEAMWORK at LE BERNARDIN.

MY FIRST JOBS WERE IN WELL-RESPECTED FRENCH RESTAURANTS WITH VERY DEFINED STRUCTURES IN THE KITCHENS. THOSE FIRST YEARS IN RESTAURANT KITCHENS ILLUSTRATED, IN AN INTENSE WAY, HOW EACH AND EVERY PERSON WHO WORKS THERE IS IMPORTANT TO THE SUCCESS OF THE BUSINESS AND THE DISHES THAT ARE SERVED. While the tasks were difficult, I believe it was essential for me to work my way through the stations of those kitchens in order to completely understand what is involved in creating great food and dining experiences. In a way, it is sort of a breaking down and building back up process—ego has to be put aside and every team member matters. There is no way a chef can do every job in a restaurant at once, so the acknowledgement of the various roles and their impact on our success is important to me.

Most days I'm at the restaurant, but when I do get out to travel and be inspired by the world and nature, I somehow always relate it back to the work we do at Le Bernardin. A trip to Sonoma County, California, was filled with visits to wineries and farms, but a friend suggested that I visit Barbara and Jacques Schlumberger. The Schlumbergers make very good wine, and have always enjoyed gardening as well. Recently, they have been distressed by the news of so many honeybee colonies dying off. Scientists haven't quite figured out why this is happening, but studies are pointing to pesticides and large-scale development that causes pollution and takes away the vegetation bees use for pollen. Barbara and Jacques decided to create a special garden, which they call "The Melissa Garden," to act as a bee sanctuary. They planted vegetation that bees especially like and designed the garden to ensure there would be flowers all year round. Barbara explained that by having a constant varied diet, the bees stay much healthier.

While at The Melissa Garden, I learned that each hive is its own community and that every bee has a very distinct job within that community. Of course there is the queen whose sole responsibility is to lay eggs—thousands and thousands of eggs to perpetuate the community. Some bees are worker bees with various roles that include cleaning the hive or feeding the larvae that will grow to become new bees. The worker bees switch roles and eventually will become the bees that get to go outside the hive and fly around collecting the pollen that will be brought back to make honey. It is important to recognize that, while the bees are flying from flower to flower collecting pollen, they are at the same time fertilizing the plants so that they will continue to grow and create fruit and vegetables. Without pollinators, like honeybees, vegetation would die, including all of the fruits and vegetables that we eat.

Jacques and I put on beekeeper's netting and gloves before he took me to look inside the actual hives while the bees were working. It was incredible to see and hear the thousands of bees. The special hives have frames that allow the bees to create very organized structures of wax cells. Some cells will house the larvae and others will store honey. Bees make lots and lots of honey—more than they need—which is why collecting honey for human consumption does not hurt the community of bees. Seeing the hives and bees close-up, feeling the weight of the frames filled with wax and honey, and hearing the buzzing was energizing. It was so inspiring to hear about how the bees work together to create a healthy colony with a good future for production. Witnessing the garden and the bees and hearing about the colonies and how they are structured caused me to reflect on how connected we all really are. Everything we do affects something or someone else. For me, it is important to be reminded of this on a personal level, but also with regard to my work. The experience made me think about the structure that we have in place at Le Bernardin and how the importance of each job in the restaurant ensures the health and success of the business.

The life of a restaurant is very complex. Inside our operation in Midtown Manhattan, there are more than 130 employees who do everything from answering phones and taking reservations to purchasing and accounting. There is the cooking, of course, and the cleaning, and also the very important job of the dining room staff that makes our customers feel welcome and well served. We could not function properly without the entire team. A very important figure in the restaurant is my business partner, Maguy Le Coze, who opened Le Bernardin along with her late brother, Chef Gilbert Le Coze, in 1986. Maguy is the soul of the restaurant—the queen, if you will—and it is her business sense and impeccable

GARDENING FOR BEES

Even if you are not a beekeeper, you can do your part to help bees thrive. It is very important to acknowledge that the use of pesticides, even in our yards, is one of the factors affecting the health of pollinating insects. Eliminate the use of home pesticides when possible. Remember that other insects besides bees help to pollinate fruits and vegetables. Many culinary herbs and ornamental plants are honeybee favorites. Whether you have a large space or a small kitchen garden, planting some of these plants will help feed the bees and nourish their colonies: asters, basil, chamomile, clover, coriander, cornflowers, dahlias, lavender, mint, poppies, rosemary, sunflowers and thyme. Find out more about gardening for bees by visiting The Melissa Garden website, www.themelissagarden.com.

with JACQUES SCHLUMBERGER, inspecting a hive.

taste that continues to breathe life into what we do in the kitchen. I have a wonderful staff of chefs, line cooks and kitchen workers who take care of the food and prepare, with exacting standards, the dishes on our menu every day. Exceptional wine service is recognized at Le Bernardin, thanks to our team of sommeliers, and the restaurant has been heralded for outstanding service in the dining room. All of the people who do the dirty work—the cleaning, the dishwashing, and the management of the garbage—work very hard and make it easier for all of us to do our jobs. Standing in the kitchen for a moment, at the peak of service, feels very much like observing the beehive at The Melissa Garden. It's tough work and the employees are strong, like the bees, but like the fragility of the wax structures within those hives, it is all a delicate balance. Witnessing the bees at the Schlumbergers' garden helped me to recognize how important our community is.

I seldom travel to a place that does not provide me some sort of inspiration in my cooking. Creating new recipes is how I express myself. Honey is one of nature's great gifts to us. It is a miracle, really, and while you might expect that bees need to be in the country to thrive, even in New York City there are rooftop beehives. You can find Manhattan honey in some of the farmers' markets that set up weekly all over the city. I like to use honey as a very distinct sweetener in dishes that might need something other than the raw taste of regular sugar. When I got back to my home kitchen, I thought it might be nice to glaze some carrots with honey and make a little sauce using honey in the pan juices from a duck breast that I cooked. The result was delicious because the slight gamey taste of duck, along with the rich sauce that was made from the rendered duck fat, needed just a bit of sweetness to lift it up. Both the earthy carrots and the duck breast were cooked with some pretty strong spices, like cumin, cayenne and coriander. Orange juice provided some acid, which was cut slightly with some butter and more honey. It turned out to be a delicious recipe that had me thinking about the bees and their important role in our lives and the health of our community.

FORMS OF HONEY

Sometimes you will see honey in clear jars looking like liquid gold. The colors of honey can vary depending on where it is from and the main type of blossom where the bees collected pollen. That's why some honey jars have names like Tupelo honey or orange blossom honey—it is because the primary source of the pollen was from a tupelo tree or an orange tree. You might also see honey in different forms:

Comb Honey–Honey inside of the honeycomb in its original form. The beeswax comb is edible.

Cut Comb Honey–Cut comb honey is liquid honey that has added chunks of the honeycomb in the jar.

Liquid Honey–Free of visible crystals, liquid honey is extracted from the honeycomb by centrifugal force, gravity, or straining. Most of the honey produced in the United States is sold in the liquid form.

Naturally Crystallized Honey–Naturally crystallized honey is honey in which part of the glucose content has spontaneously crystallized. It is safe to eat.

DUCK BREAST with
ORANGE-HONEY GLAZED CARROTS

HONEY FROM the BEES
at THE MELISSA GARDEN.

THE CREW SUITS UP to FILM the BEES at CLOSE RANGE.

THE MELISSA GARDEN. SONOMA COUNTY, CALIFORNIA.

SPICE-CRUSTED DUCK BREAST
WITH ORANGE-HONEY GLAZE AND CUMIN-SCENTED CARROTS

My visit to a bee sanctuary in Sonoma, California inspired me to start cooking more with honey. It is a versatile ingredient that adds a nice, floral sweetness.

SERVES 4

CUMIN-SCENTED CARROTS

1½ *pounds baby carrots, peeled*
2 *tablespoons unsalted butter*
1 *teaspoon honey*
⅓ *cup water, approx.*
1 *teaspoon ground cumin*
– *pinch of cayenne pepper*
– *fine sea salt and freshly ground black pepper*
½ *lemon*

SPICED DUCK BREAST

1 *teaspoon ground coriander*
½ *teaspoon ground cumin*
½ *teaspoon ground star anise*
½ *teaspoon ground white pepper*
– *pinch of cayenne pepper*
4 *(6- to 8-ounce) boneless duck breast halves, trimmed*
– *fine sea salt*
1 *tablespoon canola oil*
2 *shallots, thinly sliced*
½ *cup fresh orange juice*
¼ *cup fresh lemon juice*
1 *tablespoon honey*
2 *tablespoons unsalted butter*

Place the carrots in a large skillet with the butter, honey, and about ⅓ cup of water. Heat over medium-high heat and season the carrots with cumin, cayenne, salt and pepper. Cook, stirring occasionally, until the carrots are lightly caramelized and tender, about 20 minutes. Finish the carrots with freshly squeezed lemon juice.

Stir together the coriander, cumin, star anise, white pepper and cayenne pepper in a small bowl to blend. Season the duck breasts on both sides with salt, then coat the skin side of the duck breasts with the spice mixture, forming a crust.

Divide the canola oil between 2 sauté pans and heat over medium heat. When the pans are hot, gently place 2 duck breasts, skin sides down, in each pan. Lower the heat to medium-low and cook until the skin is golden brown and crispy, 12 to 15 minutes. Turn the duck breasts over and continue cooking for 3 to 4 minutes for medium-rare. Transfer the duck breasts to a cutting board to rest. Return the pans to the stove.

Divide the shallots between the pans and cook over medium heat until soft, about 5 minutes. Add the orange juice, lemon juice and honey, dividing equally. Simmer to reduce by half, about 8 minutes. Finish the pan sauce by whisking in the butter and seasoning to taste with salt. Combine the sauce into one pan.

Thinly slice the duck breasts crosswise and place the duck slices on 4 plates. Spoon some of the sauce over the duck and serve with the roasted carrots.

WINE PAIRINGS

Honey is a fantastic product that not only provides incredible flavor and sweetness, but also is healthy. The honey-glazed duck breast recipe pairs very well with both the Trimbach Gewurztraminer, which is always very food friendly, and the Carmenere from Errazuriz made in Chile.

TRIMBACH, GEWURZTRAMINER, CUVÉE DES SEIGNEURS DE Ribeaupierre 2000/01. Alsace, France

Gewurztraminers are quite special and very food-friendly wines. The style associated with the house is one of dry structure, flavorsome with firm acidity where appropriate. Trimbach produces an excellent Gewurztraminer, with the highest expression of the variety chez Trimbach being the Cuvée des Seigneurs de Ribeaupierre. Although the variety in question tends towards fatter, low acid wines, the wine here is a very ripe, yet still dry, aromatic style.

ERRAZURIZ, SINGLE VINEYARD CARMENÉRE 2008. Aconcagua Vallery, Chile

Carmenére ripens late in the season therefore you will find some herbaceous tones over the ripe tomato-like flavor. The very consistent weather and long ripening period in Chile's central valley are superb conditions that contribute to growing great fruit. When produced from grapes at optimal ripeness, the wine will possess a dark berry flavor with smoky (tobacco), earthy notes and a deep crimson color.

CALIFORNIA BEE STING   MAKES 4 COCKTAILS

This is a honey-based cocktail with a "sting" that comes from the chili-infused syrup.
The addition of citrus adds a fresh acidity and, of course, the vodka finishes it off.

½	cup honey
¼	cup water
½	teaspoon dried hot red chili flakes
1	orange, juiced
2	lemons, juiced
1	lime, juiced
–	ice cubes
8	ounces vodka
4	lemon peel strips, for garnish

Combine the honey, water and chili flakes in a small saucepan and bring to a boil over high heat. Remove the pan from the heat and let infuse for 15 minutes. Strain the honey syrup through a fine-mesh sieve. Set the honey syrup aside to cool completely.

In a small container, stir together the orange juice, lemon juice and lime juice.

For each cocktail, fill a cocktail shaker halfway with ice and add 2 ounces of vodka, 1½ ounces of the honey syrup and ½ ounce of the citrus juices. Cover, shake well and strain into a rocks glass filled with fresh ice. Garnish with a lemon peel strip and serve.

BUTTER LETTUCE SALAD
WITH TARRAGON AND CITRUS-HONEY VINAIGRETTE   SERVES 4

Butter lettuce is such a delicious variety of lettuce. The sturdy green leaves are sold in individual heads that are so small each diner can eat an entire head. All that is needed is a well-seasoned, well-balanced vinaigrette to complement it.

1	lemon, zested and juiced
1	lime, zested and juiced
1	tablespoon honey
1	teaspoon Dijon mustard
–	fine sea salt and freshly ground black pepper
6	tablespoons canola oil
3	heads butter lettuce (also known as Boston lettuce or Bibb lettuce)
½	cup cut fresh tarragon leaves

Whisk the lemon zest and juice, lime zest and juice, honey and mustard in a bowl and season to taste with salt and pepper. Slowly drizzle in the canola oil while whisking constantly until completely emulsified.

Trim off the core from each head of lettuce and separate the leaves, discarding the tough outer leaves. Rinse the lettuce leaves in a bowl of cold water and spin dry. Place the lettuce leaves in a large bowl and season with salt and pepper. Add the tarragon leaves and gently toss the lettuce with enough vinaigrette to coat lightly.

Stack the lettuce leaves on 4 plates, starting each stack with the large outer leaves on the bottom and ending with the small inner leaves on top. Serve immediately.

FIVE-SPICE CRUSTED VENISON TENDERLOIN
WITH CARAMELIZED HONEY-SOY GLAZE SERVES 4

Venison is a delicious underutilized meat and a nice diversion from beef or pork. The combination of five-spice powder with honey and soy makes a nice, strong seasoning that stands up to the hearty flavor of venison. While it may not be available at most supermarkets, there are some good farm-raised sources of venison available on the Internet or at gourmet markets.

½ cup honey
3 tablespoons soy sauce
3 tablespoons water
2 tablespoons rice wine vinegar
3 tablespoons unsalted butter
4 6-ounce venison tenderloin fillets
1 tablespoon Chinese five-spice powder
– fine sea salt and freshly ground
    black pepper
3 tablespoons canola oil
2 tablespoons olive oil
3 bunches scallions

Preheat the oven to 400°F.

Place the honey in a small saucepan over medium heat and simmer until caramelized to a deep golden brown color, being careful not to burn the honey, about 8 to 10 minutes. Remove the pan from the heat and stir in the soy sauce, water and vinegar. At this point the honey may harden; if it does, return the pan to the stove and gently cook the mixture over low heat until it is fully dissolved. Add the butter and whisk the glaze until fully blended.

Meanwhile, generously season the venison tenderloins with the five-spice powder, salt and pepper. Heat the canola oil in a large ovenproof sauté pan over high heat. Carefully place the venison in the pan and sear until golden on all sides, about 2 minutes per side. Brush the seared venison with some of the glaze and place the pan in the oven. Cook for about 5 minutes for medium-rare. Transfer the venison to a cutting board and let rest for at least 5 minutes.

While the venison is resting, return the pan to the stove and heat the olive oil in the pan over high heat. Add the scallions and sauté until wilted and tender, about 4 minutes. Season to taste with salt and pepper.

Divide the scallions onto 4 plates. Slice each venison tenderloin into 3 to 4 slices and shingle the slices on top of the scallions. Spoon the glaze over and around the plate. Serve immediately.

SPICED BUTTERNUT SQUASH
WITH CHESTNUT HONEY SERVES 4

Baking butternut squash instead of boiling it really brings out the earthy flavor and keeps it from getting soggy. The coating of honey and seasonings adds just the right flavor and helps the squash caramelize.

1 butternut squash,
    approx. 2- to 2½-pounds
3 tablespoons unsalted butter, melted
2 tablespoons chestnut honey
1½ teaspoons cracked black
    peppercorns
½ teaspoon ground ginger
½ teaspoon cayenne pepper
½ teaspoon ground nutmeg
– fine sea salt

Preheat the oven to 400°F.

Peel the butternut squash, cut it in half lengthwise and remove the seeds. Cut the squash into 1-inch pieces and transfer them to a shallow baking dish. Toss the squash with the butter, honey, peppercorns, cayenne, ginger and nutmeg and season to taste with salt.

Bake the squash until it is tender and caramelized, 30 to 40 minutes.

BUTTERMILK-HERB BATTERED QUAIL
WITH HONEY MUSTARD   SERVES 4

Quail dipped in buttermilk, then dredged through herb-infused flour, makes a perfect crust
for the tiny birds. Two whole quail for each person should be the perfect serving.

8   *cups canola oil*
¼   *cup Dijon mustard*
¼   *cup honey*
1   *cup buttermilk*
1   *large egg*
1½ *teaspoons cracked black peppercorns*
1   *teaspoon herbes de Provence*
    (recipe follows)
1   *cup all-purpose flour*
½   *teaspoon baking soda*
½   *teaspoon fine sea salt plus*
    more for seasoning
8   *quails, deboned and split in half*
–   *freshly ground black pepper*

Heat canola oil in a deep pot over medium heat until a deep-fry thermometer registers 350°F. Alternatively, you can use an electric deep-
fryer and set the temperature to 350°F.

Meanwhile, mix the Dijon mustard and honey in a small bowl to blend
and set it aside. Whisk the buttermilk, egg, cracked peppercorns and
herbes de Provence in a large bowl to blend. Sift together the flour,
baking soda and ½ teaspoon of salt into a medium bowl. Fold the flour
mixture into the buttermilk mixture.

Season the quail halves with salt and pepper. Working with 2 to 3
quails at a time, dip them into the batter then let the excess batter drip
off, and carefully place the battered quail into the hot oil, making sure
not to overcrowd the pot. Fry the quail until they are golden brown
and crispy, 8 to 10 minutes. Drain the fried quail on a tray lined with
paper towels.

Serve the quail with the honey mustard sauce.

HERBES DE PROVENCE   MAKES ABOUT ¼ CUP

Herbes de Provence is a blend of dried herbs reflecting those most commonly used in southern
France. It is typically sold in the spice aisle at grocery stores and is easily made from a mixture
of readily available dried herbs, allowing you to blend them according to your taste.

1   *tablespoon dried basil*
1   *tablespoon dried marjoram*
1   *tablespoon dried summer savory*
1   *tablespoon dried thyme*
1   *teaspoon dried lavender*
1   *teaspoon fennel seeds*
1   *dried bay leaf, crushed*

Combine all the ingredients in a coffee/spice grinder or blender and
pulse once or twice to combine, being careful not to grind the herbs
too fine.

CORNMEAL BISCUITS WITH WHIPPED HONEY BUTTER

These biscuits are part cornbread, part biscuit. The cornmeal provides great flavor and texture, and the whipped butter with honey makes a slightly sweet accompaniment.

MAKES 8-10

¾	cup cornmeal
1½	cups all-purpose flour
1	tablespoon sugar
2	teaspoons baking powder
¼	teaspoon fine sea salt
8	tablespoons cold unsalted butter, diced
1	cup cold buttermilk

WHIPPED HONEY BUTTER
MAKES 1 CUP

8	ounces softened unsalted butter
3	tablespoons honey
½	teaspoon fine sea salt

Preheat the oven to 425°F.

Place the cornmeal in a food processor bowl. Sift together the flour, sugar, baking powder and salt and add to the cornmeal. Pulse the cornmeal mixture once to blend. Add the cold butter and pulse until the mixture resembles coarse meal. Add ¾ cup of the buttermilk and process just until the dough starts to come together, adding more buttermilk as needed. Do not overwork the dough!

Turn the dough out onto a floured surface. Gather the dough and pat it into a rectangle that is about ½-inch thick. Using a 3-inch-diameter biscuit cutter, cut out 8 to 10 rounds. To ensure the biscuits rise properly, flour the cutter before cutting out each biscuit and do not twist the cutter. Place the biscuits, barely touching, on a baking sheet and bake until the biscuits are golden brown, 10 to 12 minutes.

For the whipped honey butter, use an electric mixer on high speed. Whip the softened butter, honey and salt in a bowl until fluffy.

118

GRILLED FIGS WITH HONEY-MASCARPONE CREAM

Figs are such a special fruit. Available in late summer, they possess a natural sweetness that turns robust when cooked. Honey and figs complement each other beautifully—it's no wonder the honey-mascarpone cream and the grilled figs make ideal companions in this dessert.

SERVES 4

- 4 *thin wooden or bamboo skewers*
- 8 *large ripe fresh figs, halved lengthwise*
- 1 *tablespoon extra virgin olive oil*
- 6 *tablespoons honey, divided*
- ½ *cup mascarpone cheese*
- ¼ *cup heavy cream*
- ½ *cup skinned roasted hazelnuts, lightly crushed*
- 1 *thyme sprig, leaves removed from stem*

Preheat the grill over high heat. Soak the skewers in water for at least 30 minutes to prevent them from scorching. Slide 4 fig halves onto each skewer, alternating each (top next to bottom) so that the fruit is fairly tight and the cut sides of the figs are facing one direction. Brush or drizzle the figs with the olive oil and 2 tablespoons of the honey.

Place the skewers on the grill, cut sides down, and cook for 2 to 3 minutes. Meanwhile, gently whisk together the mascarpone, heavy cream and 2 tablespoons of the honey.

Carefully remove the skewers from the grill and arrange them on a platter or 4 individual serving plates. Spoon some of the mascarpone mixture and the remaining 2 tablespoons of honey over and around the figs, and finish with the crushed hazelnuts and thyme leaves. Serve warm.

HONEY GRANOLA

One of my favorite things to eat for breakfast is dried fruit and yogurt. This granola is made with honey as the sweetener and is full of seeds, nuts and dried fruit. Try it with yogurt or by itself as a snack.

MAKES 5 CUPS

- 2 *cups rolled oats*
- ½ *cup bran flakes*
- ½ *cup wheat germ*
- ½ *cup mixed seeds, such as flax, pumpkin, sesame, and sunflower*
- ½ *cup nuts, such as almonds, hazelnuts, pistachios, and walnuts*
- 1 *teaspoon fine sea salt*
- 3 *tablespoons canola oil*
- ¾ *cup honey*
- ½ *cup mixed dried fruits, such as raisins, cherries, and apricots*

Preheat the oven to 300°F. Line a baking sheet with parchment paper.

Combine the oats, bran, wheat germ, seeds, nuts and salt in a large bowl. Pour in the canola oil and stir to coat. Drizzle in the honey and mix thoroughly. Spread the mixture evenly over the prepared baking sheet.

Bake the granola, stirring occasionally, for 25 to 30 minutes or until golden brown. Remove the granola from the oven, fold in the dried fruits, then spread the granola out again. Let the granola cool completely, breaking up any large pieces. The granola will keep, stored in airtight containers and placed in a cool and dry place, for up to 1 month.

119

Chapter 6

CATCH AND COOK

Cayman Islands

LOCAL FISHERMAN along the SHORES
of GRAND CAYMAN'S "7 MILE BEACH."

SOME OF THE MOST BEAUTIFUL ISLANDS IN THE CARIBBEAN SEA ARE GRAND CAYMAN, CAYMAN BRAC AND LITTLE CAYMAN. I was first introduced to the islands several years ago when Mike Ryan and The Ritz-Carlton, Grand Cayman approached me about the possibility of opening a restaurant there. After taking a trip to see the space and imagining what it could potentially be, I realized that the place was not only gorgeous but full of friendly people and natural resources that were an inspiration to me. I decided to take up the challenge and open Blue, my restaurant located inside The Ritz-Carlton on Grand Cayman Island.

The very first thing that I had to do in Grand Cayman was explore a little bit so that I could get to know the local culture and see what kinds of foods were available. For many years, the Cayman Islands have been a top destination for scuba divers. Just beneath the waters around the islands are shallow reefs and big wall drop-offs that host an incredible variety of sea life. Because of this underwater terrain, numerous shipwrecks have occurred over the years. Divers love to explore these old shipwrecks as well as the intricate reefs, and a true scuba culture thrives on the island.

The Caymanian people are very laid-back and friendly. Taking some time to get to know them has allowed me to get a glimpse of what their daily lives are like and has provided some great dialog about island food. For me, it is always fun to talk to local people and venture out on my own to explore.

Because I was opening a restaurant in Grand Cayman, I needed to find the local fish markets to see what was being caught and sold there. A few fishermen can always be found at one of the open-air markets on the island, but it is not something that can be counted on when you are shopping for a restaurant. It is very important to me that we serve as many local ingredients as possible at Blue. I had to make connections and forge friendships with the actual fishermen so that they could deliver their catch directly to the restaurant. The same goes for the farmers on the island who bring us the local produce. Much of the same produce that we

use in New York is available on Grand Cayman because of the weather and the 12-month growing season. There are some less familiar ingredients here as well, such as callaloo—which is a dark, leafy green full of flavor and a bit like spinach—and some interesting pumpkins and tropical vegetation, like lemongrass, breadfruit and bitter orange. Papayas, which we use in their green state as well as their ripened state, coconuts, passion fruit and all sorts of other tropical fruits, thrive here. I am happy that we can support small local fishermen and farmers. What they provide is so vital to our menu. It is fun to walk out the service door of Blue and buy fish, fruits and vegetables from the back of a pick-up truck. It's so different than New York City with its vast network of underground loading docks and corridors.

Captain Eric Rivers is a native Caymanian and has been boating and fishing here since he was a child. He was one of the first people I met, and we have been friends for about seven years now. Every time I come to the island, Eric and I try to get together and board his boat to explore the waters. He is very knowledgeable about the terrain, the ocean life and the culture, and I always learn a lot from him. He and I both love to eat fish, but we also respect the waters and the sea life that lives there. If we decide to go out fishing, it is not for sport. If we catch something, we are going to eat it. It is important to appreciate what the earth provides for us and the life of the animals that we use for food. Even if we never catch anything, it's okay. The ocean has a calming, almost meditative effect on me. When I am on the ocean I really feel the beauty and power of nature.

One of the ingredients that we use quite a lot at Blue is conch. I was familiar with conch and had used it in cooking a little bit before, but I never really knew how it was harvested and prepared in the Cayman Islands. Eric offered to take me diving for conch—somehow he knew exactly where to search for these large sea snails.

CAYMAN ISLANDS FACTS

First discovered by the famous Spanish explorer Christopher Columbus in 1503, this archipelago is located 480 miles south of Miami, 150 miles south of Cuba, and 180 miles northwest of Jamaica. Between the Cayman Islands and Jamaica lies the deepest part of the Caribbean Sea, called the Cayman Trough, with a depth of over four miles. The islands are made up of mostly limestone rock. The limestone has a limited amount of runoff, which is one of the reasons why the water around the islands is so clear and with visibility up to 120 feet deep.

The Cayman Islands are a British Overseas Territory and have their own currency. English is the official language and the people boast a multiracial and multicultural diversity. One quarter of the people are of European descent, another quarter declare African ancestry, and the rest claim mixed ancestry.

LOCAL DELIVERIES to BLUE, our RESTAURANT on GRAND CAYMAN.

I don't know how he knew where to find the right spot because the bottom of the ocean where we were fishing was covered in coral and seaweed and everything looked exactly the same. The conch themselves are very hard to see because they also are covered with sea plants and blend right in. We jumped into the water and although Eric was telling me exactly what to look for, it took me several dives down to finally get one conch. It was very hard but my adrenaline was rushing and it was exciting when I finally found a couple. This is something that is easy for a native to do because they have been practicing since they were children. They know their environment and it serves them well.

We found three conch in about 15 minutes and that, we decided, would be enough for us to make a nice ceviche. Back on the boat, we put out the fishing rods for a little while to see if there were any fish we could catch to eat with our conch. The water was so refreshing and beautiful that we weren't really too concerned with catching something, but if we did, we would make something to eat with it for sure. The point of our fishing was not to play with the life of the animal but to catch our lunch. We kept the line in the water for a long time and finally we did catch something. It was a blackfin tuna, a type of tuna that is common in these waters. These tuna never get very big and they are not on any endangered list. It was a beautiful fish—silver with some black tips on its fins. We reeled it in and headed for Cayman Kai, an incredible beach with a huge sandbar that reaches far out into the sea.

Once we were at Cayman Kai, we dropped the anchor and Eric took out one of the small tables from the boat. We set up a little cooking and eating area far out onto the sandbar and secured the table in the sand. The water was only about a foot and a half deep. I took out my knives and a small bowl with some ingredients that I had brought along to prepare a simple lunch with any fish we had the fortune

CAYMAN ISLANDS FACTS

There are 3 islands: Grand Cayman, Little Cayman and Cayman Brac.
–**Grand Cayman Island** is the largest of the three islands. George Town is the largest town in the country and the island is the home of Seven Mile Beach, a gorgeous stretch of pristine beach.
–**Cayman Brac** is home to around 2,000 people and is the most rugged of the islands. Boasting a limestone bluff, caves and a dramatic landscape, the island is a great place to explore nature.

–**Little Cayman** is the least populated (around 200 people live on the island) and the least developed of the three islands. It is only 10 miles long and a mile wide. There are lagoons to swim in and sparsely populated beaches to enjoy. The Caymanian people are very proactive in protecting the ocean and its resources. While tourism is a big part of the island's revenue stream, it is not the main focus of local interest. The tourists and scuba divers that come back year

after year keep coming because of the same natural beauty and genuine hospitality that I have experienced and been inspired by. I am very grateful to the people of the Cayman Islands and thankful for the natural resources on the islands. The islanders' practice of balancing a good life and their concern for the environment is a good example to follow.

SNORKELING for CONCH.

CAPTAIN ERIC RIVERS with FRESH CONCH.

to find. First we needed to extract the conch meat from the shell. The snail uses a suction method to keep itself tightly inside the shell; if that vacuum seal is compromised, the snail will not be able to maintain its strong hold. Eric used the point of one conch shell and some strong force to break a hole into the back of the other shell. This hole would make it impossible for the snail to use the suction to hold it inside. Using a large screwdriver, Eric showed me how to dislodge the meat from inside the shell. Once the vacuum seal was broken, the meat was easy to pull out. The conch meat was very similar in texture to some of the other creatures we cook at Le Bernardin—a bit slippery and firm like any other muscle. Eric demonstrated how to cut it up and then had me taste it. It is interesting how, even though I use a knife in my job every day, a new ingredient and new technique can make me feel like a beginner. After the second conch, my technique improved and I started to make the ceviche with just a little bit of lime, onion, coconut, habañero chili, cilantro, and a bit of olive oil, salt and pepper. The tuna we caught was such a beautiful fish that I encouraged Eric to start eating some as sashimi. When the fish is so fresh, sometimes the best way to eat it is raw. I sliced the tuna into very thin pieces and we ate it simply with soy sauce and wasabi. Our lunch was delicious and just the right amount for two.

The lunch that we prepared made me think about how easy it could be to cook something this simple at home. No, there is no Caribbean Sea right outside our homes, but there are good markets with fresh ingredients. The point is, when we are forced to be innovative, that may be where the greatest dishes and ideas come from. A simple ceviche or grilled lobster becomes special with just a handful of ingredients and, of course, the memory of a morning spent on pristine water with a good friend.

CAYMAN Kai.

GAIL SIMMONS inspects the FRESH, SPINY LOBSTER.

SUNSET DINNER with MIKE RYAN of
the RITZ CARLTON GRAND CAYMAN
and FRIENDS.

RUM PUNCH

Tropical places mean fun tropical drinks made with rum, pineapple, coconut and lime. Ginger beer gives this punch a bit of a kick.

MAKES 8 COCKTAILS

1½ cups dark rum
1 bottle ginger beer, 12-ounce
1 cup fresh coconut water
1 cup fresh pineapple juice
½ cup fresh lime juice
1 lime, thinly sliced
4 cups ice cubes or cracked ice
– freshly grated nutmeg

Mix the rum, ginger beer, coconut water, pineapple juice, lime juice and lime slices in a large pitcher. Stir in the ice. Pour the punch into Collins glasses and top each with a pinch of nutmeg.

GREEN PAPAYA SALAD

The julienned flesh of a green papaya has a nice crunchy texture and is not as sweet as the familiar orangey-pink ripe papaya fruit. The flavor mixes well with green onions, sweet carrot, and jalapeño pepper dressed with lime, rice wine vinegar, mint and ginger.

SERVES 4

1 large green papaya, peeled, seeded, and julienned
1 small carrot, peeled and julienned
2 scallions, thinly sliced
1 jalapeño, seeded and thinly sliced
¼ cup fresh cilantro, julienned
¼ cup fresh mint leaves, julienned
¼ cup fresh lime juice
2 tablespoons rice wine vinegar
2 teaspoons minced fresh ginger
2 teaspoons sugar
1 teaspoon mirin
– fine sea salt and freshly ground black pepper

Combine all of the ingredients in a large bowl, seasoning to taste with salt and pepper. Toss to coat evenly. Let the salad marinate for 10 minutes in the refrigerator before serving.

135

CONCH CEVICHE

Lots of people have only tried conch meat in fritters, but fresh conch meat is mild and sweet, perfect for eating raw and in ceviche. Marinated in a little bit of lime and mixed with some onion and herbs, the conch is light and fresh and briny in flavor.

SERVES 4

12 *ounces conch, cleaned*
 – *fine sea salt and freshly ground*
    white pepper
 – *piment d'Espelette*
 1 *small tomato, peeled, seeded and diced*
 ¼ *cup fresh coconut water (optional)*
 ¼ *cup thinly sliced red onion*
 ½ *jalapeño chili, seeded and minced*
 ½ *Scotch bonnet pepper, seeded and*
    minced (optional)
 3 *tablespoons julienned fresh cilantro*
 1 *tablespoon julienned fresh mint*
 3 *limes*
 2 *tablespoons extra virgin olive oil*
 – *grilled country bread*

Thinly slice the conch and place it in a large bowl. Generously season the conch with salt, pepper and piment d'Espelette. Add the diced tomato, coconut water, onion, jalapeño, Scotch bonnet, cilantro and mint, then toss lightly to combine. Squeeze the limes over the conch and toss lightly. Add the olive oil to the ceviche and toss again.

Divide the ceviche among small bowls and serve with grilled country bread.

CONCH FRITTERS WITH MANGO CHUTNEY

These fritters are made with a yeast batter that is allowed to rise before frying, resulting in a pillow-like texture. The chutney makes a refreshing accompaniment with a little bit of heat.

SERVES 4 TO 6

½ tablespoon active dry yeast
¼ cup warm water (about 95°F)
¾ cup warm whole milk (about 95°F)
1 large egg, beaten to blend
2 tablespoons olive oil
¾ cup chopped conch
¼ cup finely diced red bell pepper
1 green onion, thinly sliced
2 tablespoons chopped fresh Italian parsley
1 garlic clove, minced
– pinch of dried hot red chili flakes
1½ cups all purpose flour, sifted
– fine sea salt and freshly ground
     black pepper
– canola oil for deep frying
1 lemon, cut in wedges
– Mango Chutney (recipe follows)

MANGO CHUTNEY
MAKES 1 CUP

½ cup sugar
⅓ cup white wine vinegar
1 mango, peeled, pitted, and
     cut into ¼-inch dice
1 small shallot, minced
1 teaspoon grated fresh ginger
¼ teaspoon mustard powder
1 hot red chili such as birds eye or
     ½ Scotch bonnet, seeded and minced
– fine sea salt

Dissolve the yeast in the warm water in a medium bowl and let sit until foamy, about 10 minutes. Whisk in the milk, egg and olive oil. Stir in the conch, bell pepper, green onion, parsley, garlic and chili flakes. Season to taste with fine sea salt and freshly ground pepper Then add all of the flour and just barely mix into the wet ingredients. The mixture should still be lumpy. Let the batter rise at room temperature for at least 30 minutes.

Pour enough oil into a deep pot so that it reaches a depth of about 3 inches. Heat the oil over medium heat until a deep-fry thermometer registers 350°F. Alternatively, you can use an electric deep-fryer and set the temperature to 350°F.

Drop tablespoons of the batter into the hot oil and fry until golden brown and crispy, turning as necessary, about 4 to 6 minutes. Transfer the fritters to a baking sheet lined with paper towels to drain any excess oil.

Serve the fritters immediately with lemon wedges and spiced mango chutney.

For the mango chutney, combine the sugar and vinegar in a medium saucepan and bring to a boil. Simmer the mixture until the sugar is fully dissolved. Add the mango, shallot, chili, ginger and mustard. Cook, uncovered, until slightly thickened, 10 to 15 minutes. Season to taste with salt.

137

GRILLED SPINY LOBSTER WITH TROPICAL VIERGE

Spiny lobsters are impressive creatures. This warm water cousin to Maine lobsters does not have any large claws but does have extremely long antennae. They are delicious grilled and easy to prepare. Feel free to substitute Maine lobsters if you are not lucky enough to obtain the spiny lobsters.

SERVES 4

- ½ cup chopped mixed fresh herbs, such as chervil, chives, mint, and Italian parsley
- ½ cup extra virgin olive oil
- ¼ cup diced peeled pitted mango, about ¼-inch dice
- ¼ cup diced peeled seeded green papaya, about ¼-inch dice
- 1 tomato, peeled, seeded, and cut into ¼-inch dice
- 1 tablespoon chopped capers
- 1 tablespoon minced shallot
- 2 teaspoons finely chopped fresh ginger
- ½ garlic clove, minced
- – fine sea salt and freshly ground black pepper
- 2 live large spiny lobsters or 4 Maine lobsters
- ¼ cup softened unsalted butter

Combine the herbs, olive oil, mango, papaya, tomato, capers, shallot, ginger and garlic in a bowl. Season to taste with salt and pepper. Let this sauce vierge marinate until ready to serve, for at least 20 minutes.

Prepare the charcoal grill, letting the coals burn down to medium-high heat, 15 to 20 minutes.

While the grill is preheating, kill each lobster by plunging a large chef knife through the head, just above the eyes, making sure the knife goes all the way through the head. Then pull your knife in a downward motion through the eyes. The lobster is now dead. Cut the lobster evenly in half from head to tail. Remove the tomalley from the lobster bodies and, using scissors, remove the smaller legs.

Season the lobsters generously with salt and pepper and place them on the grill, shell sides down. Brush the lobsters with the butter and cook for 8 to 10 minutes, or until the meat just barely turns opaque.

Add the lime juice to the sauce vierge and adjust the seasoning.

Place the grilled lobsters on the center of 4 plates. Spoon the sauce vierge over the lobsters and serve immediately.

WINE PAIRINGS

Spiny Lobster comes from the warm waters of the Caribbean Sea and works well with tropical flavors like green papaya, mango and ginger. Crisp, fruit-driven white wines are a great pairing with this dish. Try the Bontani Moscatel Seco or the Patz & Hall Chardonnay suggested here. Alternately, a big style of Sauvignon Blanc, a Torronetz from Argentina or a more fruit-forward Chardonnay without much oak, would also work well.

BOTANI, MOSCATEL SECO 2008. Sierra de Malaga, Spain

This wine is made from old-vine Muscat of Alexandria grapes, grown on the north-facing slopes of Almachar in the Sierras de Malaga. The wine is fermented 60% in stainless steel and 40% in oak barrels, although the oak is more used as a structural helper rather then the simple oak flavor.

Dry Muscats are always great spring and summer wines because of the fragrant and delicate fruit flavor combined with the racy, crisp acid. You may find a lot of sweetness on the nose, but when you taste the wine there is very little sweetness—just enough to hold up to this pairing.

PATZ & HALL, CHARDONNAY HYDE VINEYARD 2007. Carneros, California

Chardonnay is very ease to handle in the vineyard and this is certainly a reason why wine makers look to Chardonnay, but also because it is the best selling varietal in America. For a while, people gave up on California Chardonnay because it is a varietal that takes many, many years of development and experimentation to produce a wonderful one. Now, because of many quality improvements and developmental changes, people are looking to California for expressive and fresher styles of Chardonnay while moving away form the creamy and bold styles. The Patz & Hall winery has grown to be quite a well-respected brand and their Hyde Vineyard wines are especially nice.

GRILLED ROMAINE "CAESAR"

Romaine lettuce is one of the most flavorful and crisp of all lettuces. It has a great structure, allowing us to cut the heads in half and cook them. The act of grilling gives them a deeper, earthier flavor, but the hearts stay crisp.

SERVES 4

¼ cup fresh lemon juice
2 large egg yolks
4 anchovy fillets, diced
1 tablespoon cracked black pepper
1 tablespoon Dijon mustard
1 garlic clove, sliced
½ cup extra virgin olive oil
– fine sea salt and freshly ground black pepper
1 jumbo romaine lettuce heart, quartered lengthwise and trimmed
½ cup freshly grated Parmesan cheese

Combine the lemon juice, yolks, anchovies, cracked pepper, mustard and garlic in a blender. With the blender on medium speed, slowly drizzle in the olive oil, blending until fully incorporated. Season to taste with salt. The dressing can be kept in the refrigerator for 3 days.

Preheat the barbecue or a grill pan over medium heat. When hot, rub the grill rack or pan with a lightly oiled cloth to prevent the lettuce from sticking. Lay the romaine quarters on a tray and brush them with the dressing. Place the romaine on the grill and cook for 2 to 3 minutes per side or just until nicely marked.

Arrange the grilled lettuce, cut sides up, on 4 plates and brush the tops with more dressing. Sprinkle some Parmesan on top and serve immediately.

SEARED TUNA SASHIMI SALAD WITH WASABI VINAIGRETTE

This is an elegant main course salad that presents the tuna as "tataki"—very lightly seared on the outside but raw in the center. The vinaigrette is a great blend of soy, lime, and wasabi.

SERVES 4

¼ cup fresh lime juice
2 tablespoons soy sauce
1 tablespoon wasabi paste
¼ cup olive oil
– fine sea salt and freshly ground black pepper
1 cup radish sprouts
¼ cup fresh cilantro leaves
1 green onion, thinly sliced
2 tuna steaks (each approx. 6-ounces and 1-inch thick)
3 tablespoons canola oil

Whisk the lime juice, soy sauce and wasabi in a bowl to blend. Whisking constantly, very slowly drizzle in the olive oil. Season to taste with freshly ground black pepper and salt, if needed. The vinaigrette can be made up to 2 days ahead and stored in the refrigerator.

Gently combine the radish sprouts, cilantro leaves and green onion in another bowl and keep in the refrigerator until ready to serve.

Generously season the tuna steaks with salt and pepper. Heat the canola oil in a large skillet over high heat until it just begins to smoke. Add the tuna steaks and sear until the tuna is nicely browned on the outside and rare in the center, about 1-½ minutes per side. Transfer the tuna steaks to a cutting board and slice into ¼-inch-thick slices.

Fan the tuna slices in a pinwheel pattern on 4 plates. Lightly dress the radish sprout salad with the vinaigrette and season to taste with salt and pepper. Place a small mound of the salad in the center of each plate, making sure the tuna is visible. Drizzle more of the vinaigrette over and around the tuna and salad. Serve immediately.

SEARED TUNA STEAK WITH BROCCOLI RABE AND GREEN PEPPERCORN SAUCE   SERVES 4

The addition of flavorful herbs and the green peppercorn sauce made with cognac, cream, and shallots, allows this tuna steak to become as formal as a fine beef steak.

BROCCOLI RABE

- 2   bunches broccoli rabe,
      washed and trimmed
- 3   tablespoons garlic butter (recipe follows)
- ½   cup freshly grated Parmesan cheese
- –   fine sea salt and freshly ground black pepper

TUNA AND SAUCE

- 3   tablespoons canola oil
- 4   tuna steaks (each approx. 6-ounces
      and 1-inch thick)
- 4   teaspoons herbes de Provence
- –   fine sea salt and freshly ground black pepper
- 1   shallot, minced
- 3   tablespoons canned green peppercorns,
      drained and lightly crushed
- 1   tablespoon unsalted butter
- ½   cup cognac
- ½   cup chicken stock (recipe p. 29)
- ¼   cup heavy cream

Bring a large pot of salted water to a boil. Prepare an ice bath. Cook the broccoli rabe in the boiling salted water for about 3 minutes or until wilted. Drain the broccoli rabe and immediately plunge it into the ice water. Drain again and set aside.

Preheat the broiler. Heat the canola oil in a large sauté pan over high heat. Season the steaks generously with herbes de Provence, salt and pepper. When the oil is almost smoking, turn the heat down slightly, add the tuna steaks and sear for 2 to 3 minutes or until nicely crusted and browned. Carefully turn the steaks over and continue cooking for another 2 minutes for rare. Transfer the tuna steaks to a baking sheet and set aside.

Make the sauce: Return the sauté pan to medium-high heat and add the shallot, green peppercorns and butter. Cook until lightly caramelized, about 6 to 8 minutes. Pull the pan just off the heat and carefully deglaze with the cognac (the mixture may flame up). Return the pan to the heat and boil until the alcohol cooks off, about 5 minutes. Add the chicken stock and simmer until it is reduced by half, about 5 minutes. Whisk in the cream and bring to a simmer. Season the sauce to taste with salt and pepper.

To serve: Melt the garlic butter in another large sauté pan over high heat. Add the blanched broccoli rabe and sauté until hot, about 4 minutes. Season to taste with salt and pepper, then remove the pan from the heat and sprinkle the Parmesan on top.

Place the tuna steaks under the broiler to rewarm, about 1 minute. Transfer the tuna steaks to a cutting board and slice the steaks into about 5 slices each.

Place the sliced tuna in the center of 4 plates, spoon the peppercorn sauce over and around the tuna, and serve immediately with the broccoli rabe on the side.

141

GARLIC BUTTER
MAKES ½ POUND

- 8   ounces (2 sticks) unsalted butter,
      at room temperature
- 2   tablespoons chopped fresh
      Italian parsley
- 2   tablespoons minced garlic
- 2   tablespoons minced shallot

Lightly whip the butter in a bowl until it is creamy. Mix in the parsley, garlic and shallot. Transfer the garlic butter to a tightly sealed container. The garlic butter can be kept in the refrigerator for up to 2 weeks.

GRILLED FRUIT EN PAPILLOTE

This is a really easy dish to make for friends and each serving has its own little pouch. The fruits are cooked just enough to coax out their natural sugars and allow them to caramelize a bit. The addition of a real vanilla bean is beautiful and imparts a very nice, natural vanilla flavor. Parchment paper can be used instead of foil.

SERVES 4

- 4 *rectangular aluminum foil sheets, each 12 x 8 inches*
- 4 *small apricots, halved and pitted*
- ½ *pineapple, peeled, cored, and cut into chunks*
- 16 *Bing cherries, pitted*
- ¼ *cup fresh grated coconut*
- ¼ *cup toasted shelled pistachios*
- 2 *vanilla beans, halved lengthwise*
- 4 *cinnamon sticks*
- 4 *teaspoons brown sugar*
- 4 *teaspoons unsalted butter, at room temperature*
- – *freshly ground black pepper*
- – *vanilla ice cream (recipe p. 163) or any ice cream or sorbet*
- – *fresh mint sprigs, for garnish*

In the center of each sheet of aluminum foil, place 2 apricot halves, 4 or 5 chunks of pineapple and 4 cherries. Add 1 tablespoon each of coconut and pistachios, ½ vanilla bean and 1 cinnamon stick. Top the fruit with 1 teaspoon each brown sugar and butter, finishing with a grind of black pepper to taste.

To close each package, bring the 2 longer sides of the foil together and make 2 or 3 tight folds over, about ½-inch each. Roll up the shorter sides to form a tight package around the fruit. Take care not to puncture the foil, as the primary means of cooking will be by the steam trapped inside the foil; you also want to preserve all the juices that are created.

To cook on a charcoal grill, prepare the grill, letting the coals burn down to medium heat, about 20 minutes. Adjust the grill rack to allow maximum space between the coals and the rack. Place the papillotes on the grill, close the lid, and grill-roast for 10 to 15 minutes, or until warmed through.

For a gas grill, preheat the grill to at least 400°F, then place the papillotes on the highest rack. Turn off the gas, close the lid, and allow the pouches to cook from the residual heat for 10 to 15 minutes, or until warmed through.

Allow packages to cool slightly. Open each of the packages and transfer to a bowl or plate. Top with a scoop of vanilla ice cream and a sprig of fresh mint.

Chapter 7

ARTISANAL

Mugello, Tuscany, Italy

ATTENTION TO DETAIL, THE STUDY OF THE HISTORY OF A CRAFT AND THE PURSUIT OF PERFECTION, AS WELL AS PERSONAL EXPRESSION WITHIN THAT CRAFT, ARE TRAITS THAT MAKE AN ARTISAN. As a chef, I am always intrigued with, and pleased to meet, the artists who produce specialty food products like the cheesemakers, meat curers, winemakers and brewmasters. These are the people who devote their lives to making impeccable products in small batches. Old world locations, like European towns, always seem to have a rich tradition of artisan products and shops. Instead of department stores and mega-marts, the town centers become public gathering places where open-air farmers' markets are surrounded by small shops focusing on specialty products and services. These types of stores connect a community in a special way and also feed a local, and sometimes even global, economy.

The Tuscan town of Scarperia, known for its handcrafted cutlery, is positioned close to the original Roman road that was built to take travelers from southern to northern Italy. Travelers discovered a natural spring near the road and were able to refresh themselves and fill jugs with water to take with them. The wealthy and powerful Medici family built a house near the spring in the 1500's, and terra cotta pipes, used for transporting water to the Medici home, were discovered near the source of the spring water. Much later, in the 1860's, Panna water—named after the Medici home *Villa Panna*—began to be bottled in a repurposed farmhouse and delivered by horse and cart to Florence to be sold. The water, because it travels underground—literally through the earth—possesses a minerality that brings character to its flavor. It's very much like *terroir* in wine and definitely impacts the flavors of the wine and food you have with it.

147

THE ICONIC FOUNTAIN
at VILLA PANNA

If you think about it, even animals reflect terroir because of how and what they eat. Seed saving, soil management and animal husbandry take on an artistic edge when consideration for everything—from breeding to the seasonal food that an animal receives—is put into play. Many farmers understand that even tiny changes in breeding and feeding can make a big difference in how the meat tastes, proving farmers can be artisans too.

In Mugello, Italy, a region famous for its cows and chestnuts, I visited a farm that raised their herd of cows amidst their famed chestnut trees. I was impressed with how big and healthy the cows seemed to be, and I observed that their pastures were very green and that the cattle were able to move into the hills to find cool chestnut groves to graze in. Nature also knows how to mix up an animal's diet. Pastured cows are extremely adept at finding very green grass, which is full of the nutrients that a mother cow needs in order to produce milk for her calves. Other types of plants and grasses add another level of nutrition. In the autumn, when the cattle need to bulk up for the coming winter, the chestnuts start to fall and provide fat and protein to help the cows stay healthy through the cold weather. Walking through the groves, the first thing I saw was a beautiful, brownish-red cow standing under a massive chestnut tree with her calf. As I walked around, gathering chestnuts, I was thinking about the farms I had visited while growing up in France, and how the farmers and artisans of a locality represent "authenticity." The farm and the chestnut forest were, for me, very authentic and inspiring.

In the nearby town of Marradi, a festival was being held celebrating chestnut season and also the livestock that is bred and raised in the area. Prize-winning farm animals were brought in for people to see and the farmers

SALUMI AND FORMAGGIO

Italian cured meats and cheeses are distinct—full of character and specific flavors and textures that Italian artisans have perfected over centuries. It is lots of fun to put together tasting plates of different meats and cheeses when entertaining. Here is a small guide to salumi and formaggio:

Salumi—the general term referring to salted, cured cuts of meat or sausages.

Bresaola—an air-dried, salted beef that is usually aged between 2 and 4 months. Serve bresaola sliced very thin.

Finocchiona—a type of salami that is made from pork and fat and then left to cure for 3 to 4 months. The name refers to the addition of fennel seeds (*finocchio*) in the meat mixture. Serve this salami in thick slices.

Lardo—pork fatback that is cured for several months in salt, rosemary and other herbs. Lardo di Colonatta is the most famous lardo because of its distinct flavor extracted from months of being cured inside marble tubs. Serve lardo in very thin slices with bread.

Mortadella—a sausage that is made from pork and infused subtly with seasonings, like pepper, coriander, and anise. Cubes of the high-quality fat from the jowl of the hog are introduced into the sausage, which creates a nice design when sliced. Serve mortadella in thin slices.

CHESTNUT GROVE in MUGELLO.

149

Prosciutto—a ham that has been seasoned with salt and other seasonings, then left to air dry for several months. The concentrated flavor and texture makes it an extremely popular choice. Serve prosciutto in paper-thin slices.

Gorgonzola—a creamy blue cheese made from cow or goat milk. The introduction of a particular mold and the aging process give the cheese its blue color and its strong flavor.

Mozzarella—a semi-soft cheese made from either the milk of the water buffalo (*mozzarella di bufala*) or cow's milk (*mozzarella fior di latte*). The cheese is cut into chunks or balls and stored in water or brine to keep its texture.

Parmigiano—a hard cow's milk cheese that is aged for 6 to 36 months. The most famous, Parmigiano-Reggiano, is made in a very specific region of Italy and is designated by European law as a "protected designation of origin." The

very distinct stamp on the outer rind guarantees its authenticity

Ricotta—not technically a cheese, but a by-product of the manufacture of cheese, ricotta is recooked whey (the liquid that comes from the curds when cheese is made). The smooth texture and mild flavor makes it a great cheese for cooking.

were there to talk about their work. There were men roasting chestnuts over an open flame in large cylindrical cages that they could turn with a crank. The smell was delicious and festival-goers were walking around eating warm chestnuts from paper bags. There were also artisan producers from all over Tuscany who had set up stalls, selling truffles, porcini mushrooms, and salumi (Italian cured meats) such as prosciutto, mortadella, salami and lardo. In addition to meats, I am always amazed at the wide variety of cheeses that are made.

Cheese is a product that undoubtedly takes its flavor profile from the place of origin, the type of milk, the style of the cheesemaker, length of the aging period and how it is stored—every factor makes a difference. In the region of Mugello in Tuscany, we visited Il Palagiaccio, a dairy and farm where the cows are raised on the same property where the cheese is produced. This means that there is a very close watch over the way the cows are raised, and a short time between when the cows are milked and when the milk is bottled and the cheese is made.

Dr. Luigi Bolli works at the dairy and he took me on a tour of the small but very productive business. He explained the different processes that are used to make fresh cow's milk cheese, like ricotta, and the aging processes for stronger flavored, aged cheeses. The most important step is to start with the best milk possible, which is not a problem for them since they raise the very cows that provide them with the milk. Dr. Bolli allowed me to help make some very delicious, silky ricotta cheese that was a bit of a surprise to me. The cheese was set in a mold, and when it was turned out it retained its shape. The texture was smooth and creamy—not like the grainier ricotta that comes in a tub. Just outside the sterile cheesemaking room, there is a beautiful shop where people can come in and buy a big selection of their

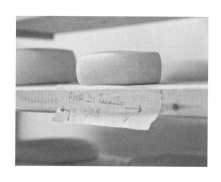

Il Palagiaccio in MUGELLO, ITALY.

THE MUGELLO VALLEY in TUSCANY.

Il Palagiaccio in MUGELLO, ITALY.

cheeses, as well as milk, yogurt and gelato. It is so nice to visit a business with a great history of farming and craftsmanship, and then be able to buy the products right on site.

I ended up buying some of the ricotta from Il Palagiaccio to take to another friend, Giovanna Carcasci, who owns Ristorante Maga Mago in Barbarino di Mugello. Giovanna invited me to come and learn how to make pasta from her—something she makes every day in her beautiful restaurant. Even though I'm a trained chef and know many different culinary techniques, there is nothing like learning a technique from an artist who practices her craft every day. Pasta looks simple until you try to make it well. There are pasta machines for sale, but the pasta never comes out as good as if it is made by hand. As Giovanna says, "It needs to feel the heat of your hand." The best pasta dishes are minimal combinations, and for the ravioli we made that day, Giovanna and I simply used ricotta, fresh spinach from the market, eggs, Parmesan, salt and pepper for the filling. Some butter and sage in the pan was all that we used to sauté the finished ravioli.

Traveling through Tuscany, I was reminded of how precious true artisan products and methods are. It is important to remember to pass along skills and information to the next generation. Back home, I was inspired to go to some local shops in New York and buy ingredients to make a pasta dish for my family. Carbonara, made from eggs and cream cooked with cured ham, has always been one of my favorite sauces. I chose some smoked bacon that reminded me of all the salumi stands in the markets. Because there are so few ingredients to the dish, it is important to buy the most delicious ingredients. For me, the walk from shop to shop was a nice reminder of all the talented people I met in Tuscany, and that authenticity is out there if we take the time to seek out dedicated artisans and shopkeepers.

MAKING RAVIOLI with GIOVANNA.

ARTICHOKE AND ESCAROLE SALAD
WITH PECORINO PESTO
162

GRILLED PORCINI MUSHROOMS WITH PECORINO
AND ROSEMARY-GARLIC OIL
163

RICOTTA GNOCCHI
WITH PROSCIUTTO, PEAS AND MINT
160

RICOTTA-SPINACH RAVIOLI
WITH BUTTER AND SAGE
161

CARBONARA
159

BISTECCA ALLA FIORENTINA
162

BROWN BUTTER ICE CREAM
VANILLA ICE CREAM
165

CHESTNUT CAKE
163

CARBONARA

Smoked bacon lardons and egg yolks mixed with crème fraîche—not cream as in the classic recipe—gives this sauce a bit of tanginess to complement the richness. The sliced chives provide a subtle flavor from the onion family.

SERVES 4

½ cup diced applewood-smoked bacon
2 cups crème fraîche
2 large egg yolks
1 teaspoon freshly ground
   black pepper
– fine sea salt
8 ounces dried linguine
1½ cups freshly grated Parmesan cheese
   plus more for garnish
4 tablespoons thinly sliced fresh chives

Bring a large pot of salted water to a boil over high heat.

Meanwhile, sauté the bacon in a large skillet over medium-low heat until crisp, about 10 minutes. Add the crème fraîche and bring to a simmer. Whisk the egg yolks into the sauce. Add the black pepper and season to taste with salt.

When ready to serve, cook the linguine in the boiling salted water until al dente. Drain the pasta and add it to the sauce. Stir in 1-½ cups of the Parmesan cheese and chives; let stand for 1 minute to allow all the flavors to blend.

Using a meat fork or carving fork, twirl a quarter of the pasta (for each serving) and place each swirl of pasta in the center of 4 bowls. Spoon some of the sauce over and around the pasta and top with more grated Parmesan cheese, as desired. Serve immediately.

WINE PAIRINGS

The wines featured are from the Veneto and Piedmont regions of Italy and two very different regions in terms of wine style as well as cultural style. The Piedmont lies in the foothills of the Alps and is the region of Italy bordered by Switzerland and France. The Nebbiolo grape is indigenous to the Piedmont and the wine selected here supplies a fresh brightness that plays against the richness of the carbonara sauce. The Garganega is made by a boutique winery in the Soave area near Verona. The artisanal wine featured here is reflective of Verona's appreciation of the arts.

TRAVAGLINI GATTINARA NEBBIOLO 2004. Piedmont, Italy

Travaglini is a family-owned wine estate that is considered one of the best—if not the best—producer in this area. This wine works very well with the carbonara because it possesses bright fruit and some fresh acid that will just cut through the richness of the cream and eggs.
The word *nebbiolo* comes from *la nebbia*, meaning "the fog." The name is appropriate because the fog here is so important for the slow, cool and long ripening phase for this grape and the harvests here often don't start before mid-October. These cool growing seasons and specific traditional cellar techniques are responsible for the fruit frequently struggling against the grape's high tannins and the sharp acid.

ANSELMI CAPITEL CROCE 2005/06. Veneto, Italy

Capitel Croce is named after the vineyard site atop of the Zoppega Hill, near the Croce Shrine in Monforte, in the Soave area of Veneto. The capital is Verona and is one of the main tourist destinations in Northeast Italy. In the surrounding areas of Verona you find a lot of agriculture and especially lots of vineyards. Roberto Anselmi took over a quite sizable and famous winery from his parents and radically changed the production from large scale to a limited production boutique winery that enjoys even more fame. Capitel Croce is made out of 100% Garganega and was fermented for 8-12 months in oak barrels. It is a dense wine with lots of fruit and a strong backbone.

RICOTTA GNOCCHI WITH PROSCIUTTO, PEAS AND MINT

Making these little potato dumplings from scratch is satisfying and a tradition in Italy. They are easy to make and can be tossed, like pasta, with many different ingredients. This simple recipe with peas, mint and prosciutto is a springtime favorite.

SERVES 4-6

2 *cup fresh shelled English peas*
1 *pound russet potatoes, baked, peeled, and put through a ricer*
½ *cup (loosely packed) grated ricotta salata*
½ *cup fresh ricotta*
2½ *cups all-purpose flour plus more for dusting*
– *freshly grated nutmeg*
– *fine salt and freshly ground white pepper*
1 *tablespoon canola oil*
3 *tablespoons extra virgin olive oil*
1 *small onion, finely diced*
1 *garlic clove, finely minced*
4 *ounces sliced prosciutto, julienned*
2 *tablespoons unsalted butter*
¼ *cup fresh mint leaves, julienned*

Bring a large pot of salt water to a boil.

Blanch the peas in boiling water for 3 to 5 minutes, until tender. Using a strainer, remove the peas from the water and transfer the strainer to an ice water bath to stop them from cooking. Strain the peas and set aside.

Change the water in the pot and bring to a boil.

Put the riced potatoes in a large bowl and spread them out to cover the bottom of the bowl. Sprinkle the grated ricotta salata and fresh ricotta evenly over the potatoes and sprinkle 2 cups of the flour over the cheese. Season to taste with nutmeg, salt and white pepper. Gently knead all of the ingredients together, using more flour as necessary, until the dough comes together but is not sticky.

Place the dough on a floured surface, cut it into 4 equal pieces, and roll out each piece into a long rope that is about ½-inch in diameter. Cut the ropes crosswise into 1-inch pieces and lightly dust with flour.

Spread the canola oil over a baking pan to coat. Working in batches, boil the gnocchi in the salted water until they float to the surface, about 2 minutes. Using a small strainer or a large slotted spoon, remove the gnocchi from the water and place them in a single layer on the oiled baking pan. Reserve about ½ cup of the cooking water.

Heat the olive oil in a large sauté pan over high heat. Add the onion and garlic and sauté until soft and just beginning to color, 4 to 5 minutes. Add the prosciutto and peas and sauté until hot. Add the blanched gnocchi, ¼ cup of the gnocchi cooking water, and the butter. Season to taste with salt and pepper and toss to coat evenly, adding more liquid as necessary. When the gnocchi are hot, toss them with the mint and serve immediately.

RICOTTA-SPINACH RAVIOLI WITH BUTTER AND SAGE

This recipe is from my friend Giovanna Carcasci in Scarperia, Italy. She owns a restaurant known for its house-made pasta, and these ravioli are delicious, cooked in a pan with just a bit of sage and butter.

SERVES 4

2 *tablespoons olive oil*
1 *garlic clove, minced*
½ *pound baby spinach, washed*
– *fine sea salt and freshly ground black pepper*
1 *cup fresh ricotta cheese*
½ *cup freshly grated Parmesan cheese plus more for garnish*
1 *large egg yolk*
– *5 to 6 fresh pasta sheets, each about 10x4 inches (see pappardelle recipe p. 26)*
1 *large egg, beaten to blend*
4 *tablespoons softened unsalted butter*
¼ *cup torn fresh sage leaves*

Heat the olive oil in a large skillet over medium heat. Add the garlic and briefly sauté until soft and aromatic. Add the spinach, season to taste with salt and pepper, and sauté until just wilted, about 3 minutes. Place the sautéed spinach in a strainer set over a bowl and drain the excess liquid. Set aside to cool. When the spinach is cool enough to handle, press down on it in the strainer to squeeze out the excess liquid.

Transfer the sautéed spinach to a cutting board and chop finely. Stir the chopped spinach, ricotta and ½ cup of the Parmesan cheese in a bowl to blend. Season to taste with salt and pepper, then stir in the egg yolk.

Line a baking sheet with parchment paper and dust the paper with flour. Lay 1 pasta sheet on a lightly floured work surface. Lightly brush the bottom half of the dough with the beaten egg. Place 5 mounds (about 1 teaspoon each) of the filling 2 inches apart in the center of the egg-washed dough. Fold the top half of the dough over the filling. Dust the top with flour. Seal the ravioli by pressing and molding the pasta over the filling, being careful to eliminate air pockets. Cut the ravioli with a pasta cutter (there should be no more than ¼-inch of pasta around the filling). Place the ravioli on the prepared baking sheet and dust the tops of the ravioli again with more flour. Repeat with the remaining sheets of pasta and filling to make about 30 ravioli total. The ravioli can be made up to 1 week ahead and kept frozen.

Bring a large pot of salted water to a boil over high heat. Cook the ravioli in the boiling salted water for 1 to 2 minutes, or until they just begin to float. Drain the ravioli and place them in a large bowl. Add the butter and sage to the bowl and toss gently to coat the ravioli. Lightly season the ravioli with salt and pepper and divide them among 4 plates. Garnish with freshly grated Parmesan cheese and serve immediately.

ARTICHOKE AND ESCAROLE SALAD
WITH PECORINO PESTO   SERVES 4

Escarole is a leafy green from the chicory family. It is crisp and just slightly bitter, which makes
it a delicious base for this salad containing earthy artichokes, bright basil pesto and lemon.

1   cup (loosely packed) basil leaves
¼   cup grated Pecorino Romano
1   teaspoon minced garlic
½   cup plus 2 tablespoons extra virgin
    olive oil
¼   cup toasted pine nuts
–   fine sea salt and freshly ground
    black pepper
1   lemon
4   large artichokes
2   tablespoons canola oil
1   head escarole, tough outer leaves
    removed, washed, and cut up
2   tablespoons fresh lemon juice

Place the basil, Pecorino, garlic, ½ cup of the olive oil and half of the pine
nuts in a mini food processor or blender. Add a pinch of salt and some freshly
ground black pepper and blend until smooth.

Fill a large bowl with water. Cut the lemon in half and squeeze the juice into
the water. Remove the artichoke stems. Using a small knife, start at the base
of the artichoke and remove the leaves. Continue removing the leaves until
all of them are gone. Next, remove all of the green flesh from the artichoke
(any green flesh left on the artichoke will turn brown while cooking). Using
a spoon, scoop out the choke of the artichoke. As you finish cleaning each
artichoke heart, immediately place it in the bowl of lemon water.

Heat the canola oil in a large skillet over high heat. Drain the artichokes well
and cut them into ¼-inch-thick slices. Add the sliced artichokes to the hot
skillet and season to taste with salt and pepper. Sauté until the artichoke slices
are golden brown and tender, 8 to 10 minutes. Remove the skillet from the
heat and set the artichokes aside until cool enough to handle.

Place the escarole in a large bowl and season with salt and pepper. Add the
sautéed artichokes and gently toss with the lemon juice and remaining 2
tablespoons of olive oil. Divide the salad among 4 plates. Spoon the pesto
over and around the salad and serve immediately.

BISTECCA ALLA FIORENTINA   SERVES 4

Florence is known for its exceptional beef. Florentine-style steak refers to a thick cut of porterhouse
steak. The simple marinade, made of a little olive oil, black pepper, lemon peel and garlic, imparts
good flavor while tenderizing the beef.

4   tablespoons olive oil
2   Porterhouse steaks (2 pounds each;
    prime dry-aged, if available)
4   garlic cloves, minced
2   tablespoons freshly cracked
    black pepper
8   lemon peel strips (from 1 lemon)
–   coarse sea salt or kosher salt
4   tablespoons unsalted butter

Drizzle the olive oil over both sides of the steaks, then rub both sides of the
steaks evenly with the garlic. Season with the cracked pepper. Place 2 lemon
peel strips on each side of the steaks. Cover and refrigerate for at least 3 hours.

Prepare the charcoal grill, letting the coals burn down to medium heat, about
15 to 20 minutes. Remove the lemon peel from the steaks and season the
steaks generously with coarse salt. Grill the steaks, making sure that the
thick strip sides of the steaks are over the hotter part of the grill, for about
5 minutes on each side for medium-rare doneness. As the steaks grill, move
them around as necessary to manage the heat of the grill. Transfer the steaks
to a platter, place 2 tablespoons of butter on top of each steak, and let rest for
at least 5 minutes.

Slice the steaks away from the bones and shingle the steak slices on plates.
Drizzle the drippings and accumulated juices over the steaks and serve.

GRILLED PORCINI MUSHROOMS
WITH PECORINO AND ROSEMARY-GARLIC OIL   SERVES 4

Porcini mushrooms were in season while I was traveling throughout Italy this past year, and the markets were full of these huge mushrooms. One of the easiest ways to cook porcini mushrooms is on the grill with olive oil and herbs. A little shave of Pecorino cheese on top finishes them off perfectly.

½ cup extra virgin olive oil
2 garlic cloves, thinly sliced
1 tablespoon minced fresh rosemary
1 pound fresh porcini mushrooms
– fine sea salt and freshly ground black pepper
1 piece Pecorino Romano, shaved with a peeler
1 lemon, cut in half
– Maldon sea salt

Combine the olive oil, garlic and rosemary in a small saucepan over low heat and simmer for 2 minutes. Remove the oil mixture from the heat and let stand 20 minutes. Strain through a coffee filter set over a fine-mesh sieve. Set the rosemary-garlic oil aside.

Preheat the grill over high heat. Trim the mushrooms and brush them clean with a brush or a damp towel. Cut the mushrooms lengthwise into about ½-inch-thick slices. Brush both sides of the mushroom slices with the rosemary-garlic oil and season lightly with fine sea salt and pepper. Grill the mushrooms until they are nicely marked and just barely cooked through, 2 to 3 minutes per side. Remove the mushrooms from the grill and arrange them on a plate.

Top the mushrooms with 5 to 6 pieces of shaved Pecorino Romano and drizzle more of the rosemary-garlic oil over the mushrooms. Finish by squeezing the lemon halves over the mushrooms and sprinkling with a few flakes of the Maldon salt.

CHESTNUT CAKE   MAKES 1 LOAF

Autumn in Tuscany is one of the most beautiful times of the year to visit. The air is clear and crisp and the chestnuts are falling off the trees. There are entire festivals held to celebrate chestnuts, and in that spirit, this recipe utilizes and pays homage to the chestnut.

2 cups sweetened chestnut purée, available in cans or tubes from gourmet markets
½ cup unsalted butter, softened
4 large egg yolks
3 large whole eggs
½ cup all purpose flour
2 teaspoons baking powder
– nonstick cooking spray

Preheat the oven to 325°F.

Using a stand mixer fitted with the paddle attachment, beat the chestnut purée and butter in the mixer bowl on medium speed until smooth. Whisk the egg yolks and whole eggs in another bowl to blend, then slowly add them to the chestnut mixture, beating to blend well. Sift the flour and baking powder into a small bowl, then add it to the chestnut mixture and beat just until blended.

Spray a 9x5x3 inch loaf pan with nonstick cooking spray and transfer the batter to the pan. Bake for 20 to 25 minutes, or until a cake tester comes out clean when inserted into the center of the cake.

163

BROWN BUTTER ICE CREAM

Michael Laiskonis, the pastry chef at Le Bernardin, loves to make ice cream. He subtly infuses the creams with interesting flavors that complement the desserts they accompany. Like this one, they are also delicious on their own.

MAKES 1 QUART

2   *cups plus 6 tablespoons heavy cream*
2   *cups nonfat milk*
1   *tablespoon nonfat dry milk powder*
¾   *cup granulated sugar*
4   *large egg yolks*

Place 2 cups of the heavy cream in a saucepan and bring to a boil. Lower the heat and allow the cream to slowly reduce until it thickens and begins to brown and separate, stirring occasionally, for about 30 minutes. As the cream begins to brown and separate, stir it continuously until the browned milk solids have clumped together and separated from the milk fat. Strain the excess fat from the solids, pressing to remove as much fat as possible.

Place the nonfat milk and browned solids in a saucepan. Whisk in the dry milk powder to rehydrate and gently bring the mixture to a boil.

Whisk the sugar and egg yolks in a large bowl to blend. Gradually whisk the hot milk mixture into the yolk mixture, a small amount at a time, so as not to curdle the yolks. Return the mixture to the saucepan and stir over low heat until slightly thickened, about 8 to 10 minutes. Remove from the heat and whisk in the remaining 6 tablespoons of heavy cream. Cover and refrigerate the custard for at least 12 hours to allow it to mature.

Process the custard in an ice cream machine according to the manufacturer's instructions. Transfer the ice cream to a container, then cover and allow it to harden in the freezer.

VANILLA ICE CREAM

MAKES 1 QUART

1   *pint whole milk*
1   *vanilla bean, split lengthwise*
1   *tablespoon nonfat dry milk powder*
10   *tablespoons granulated sugar*
4   *large egg yolks*
6   *tablespoons heavy cream*

Place the milk in a saucepan. Scrape the seeds from the vanilla bean into the milk, then add the bean to the milk. Whisk in the dry milk powder to rehydrate and gently bring to a boil. Whisk the sugar and egg yolks in a large bowl to blend. Gradually whisk the hot milk mixture into the yolk mixture, a small amount at a time, so as not to curdle the yolks. Return the mixture to the saucepan and stir constantly over low heat until slightly thickened, about 8 to 10 minutes. Remove from the heat and whisk in the heavy cream. Discard the vanilla bean. Cover and refrigerate the custard for at least 12 hours to allow the mixture to mature.

Process the custard in an ice cream machine according to the manufacturer's instructions. Transfer the ice cream to a container, then cover and allow it to harden in the freezer.

Chapter 8

PERFECT PAIRINGS

Sonoma, California

ALDO SOHM, WINE DIRECTOR at LE BERNARDIN.

BEYOND MASTERING COOKING TECHNIQUES, A REAL CHALLENGE IS BALANCING FLAVORS TO CREATE AN INSPIRED AND PLEASING DINING EXPERIENCE. Perhaps a good palate—the ability to detect flavors—is something one is just born with, or maybe it is a learned skill. Most likely it is a bit of both, but either way, the goal of any cook—and certainly of the team at Le Bernardin—is to continue to explore flavors and present them in a beautiful way to the people who visit the restaurant.

A large part of the service at Le Bernardin is our beverage program. The team of sommeliers is made up of five professionals who understand and accept the challenge of not just pairing our food with an appropriate wine, but creating an exciting and compelling pairing. The sommelier must be familiar with not only varietals and vintages but every aspect of the menu and the ingredients and flavor profiles of each dish. Once our chef team comes up with a new dish and we are ready to serve it to our clients, we make sure the beverage team has the opportunity to taste the dish and begin considering what wines will be suggested as pairings.

At Le Bernardin, both the chefs and the sommeliers believe the perfect pairing to be when the food elevates the quality of the wine and the wine does the same thing for the food. It's not just about finding a combination that is adequate; it's about making the entire taste experience better. Chefs use their knowledge of flavors combined with technique to coax a recipe into their inspired vision of a dish. Sommeliers use their vast knowledge of the technical and artistic aspects of winemaking, as well as what they know about geography, geology, weather, and even history, to dictate how they choose wines for a pairing. It is always amazing to me that a sommelier can retain so much information and then be able to relay the statistics in an interesting, approachable way. Some of it can go over my head a little bit, especially when they start talking about the real technicalities of how each wine was made, but I understand that all of that information helps them to make educated decisions. Pairing wine with food is part science and part personal, artistic expression.

Aldo Sohm is the wine director at Le Bernardin and is always up for a challenge. Recently, we gave him a very tough one when the sous chefs and I came up with a crabmeat dish that included coconut milk, lime, Thai basil, and some pretty hot chili oil. The dish was inspired by Southeast Asian flavors, and after working with the recipe for a while, we felt it was ready to make a debut and for Aldo to be thinking of some pairing options. Some of the flavors to consider were the rich sweetness of the crabmeat, the aromatic qualities of the coconut and basil, the distinct acidity of the lime, and the hot chili. Aldo tasted the dish first and then went into the cellar to do some thinking and consideration.

The wine cellar at Le Bernardin is actually a long, narrow room within the belly of the restaurant that can store 15,000 bottles of wine at the perfect holding temperature. The walls of the cellar are approximately 18 feet high and are filled on both sides with our inventory of wine. There is barely room to turn around, and tall ladders must be used to reach the top bins. Aldo and his team spend lots of time in this chilly closet, and it is there where they can take a moment in the quiet to ponder and select what they hope to be a perfect pairing.

Once Aldo took a little time to consider the crab dish, he came back to the kitchen with five different white wines and a little surprise—some sake. The sake seemed like a risk but we all agreed it might make sense and end up working. We also knew that many of our clients might be excited and open to an interesting sake pairing. However, because sake has more alcohol in it than most wines, it was too powerful and made the intensity of the dish a little too strong. Although sake was not the best choice for this dish, it was a

WINE TASTING DESCRIPTIONS

Because tasting wine is often influenced by personal preference, and because each person tastes flavors differently, there are many descriptions that may help close the gap between personal preference and the analytical system of describing a specific wine. Certainly not all of the descriptions are listed here, but these are some very common ones:

Acidity–a very general term for fresh, tart or sour taste in wine. Acidity is a major factor in the quality of the wine because it stabilizes it and plays an important role in the aging process. Acidity carries the refreshing flavors in wine and dictates a lot of the tone of a wine.

Appley–some wines have a strong green, red or yellow apple flavor, which usually comes from the malic acid in grapes—the same acid that is present in apples. These apple flavors are very typical for certain varietals.

Berrylike–grapes are berries so it is not a stretch to find that some flavor qualities of wine are reminiscent of other berries, like blackberries. Wines will generally smell of red or dark berries and the specific berry that can be detected is subjective.

Body–this term describes how wine feels in the mouth. The viscosity and density of a wine will very often be described as either full or light-bodied.

Complexity–some wines have multiple

THE VINEYARDS at IRON HORSE, SONOMA, CALIFORNIA.

layers of flavors and aromas that translate into what is described as complexity.

Earthy–this positive term is used when a wine literally has the fragrance and taste of loamy earth or a forest floor. Earthiness carries complexity with it and adds to the depth of a wine's flavor. An earthy flavor can also speak to the terroir of a wine.

Floral–this description is used when a wine is heavy with aromatics that mimic the smells of flowers. Gewurztraminer, for example, very often has the aroma of rose petals.

Jammy–when a wine has very distinct, concentrated fruit characteristics, it can be referred to as being "jammy"—as in grape or other fruit jam. Most wines described this way have lower acid levels and therefore the sensation of jam is very strong.

Minerality–a subtle characteristic in wine, commonly referring to those flavors like wet stone, flint, or oyster shells, all with a faint metallic taste. European wine makers pay especially close attention to the mineral quality in wine.

Oaky–a description that speaks to a wine's level of oak flavor or smell. The oak barrels, used in the aging process, give distinct oak flavor to wines and help to exchange hard wine tannins with soft wood tannins. Some tasters have come to enjoy and expect a certain level of oak in particular varietals.

fun diversion. As we tasted through the five different wines, some of them were immediately ruled out for various reasons. A couple of the wines were a bit acidic and made the lime too strong and instantly made the spiciness of the chili oil more pronounced. Aldo suspected that we needed a wine with a bit of residual sugar to help coat the throat and not cover the spice but soften it a bit. In the end, we chose a Traminer from Stéphane Tissot, which is made in Jura, France—it was a perfect pairing.

All this exploration of the science of wine and the art of pairing makes me want to know more. I love sparkling wine and have always wanted to see the process of making it. Laurence and Joy Sterling, the brother and sister team that runs Iron Horse Vineyards in Sonoma, California, invited me to their winery to see the special process that grapes must go through to make sparkling wine and to explore how to think about pairing it with food.

Laurence took me into their winery where the wine is made and stored. Inside, there were hundreds of filled bottles being held upside down in special racks. The yeast in the bottles and the process of holding it there determine much of the taste and make the wine sparkle. Joy explained that the goal is to get the tiniest pinpoint bubbles to be present. The bubbles create that very special effervescent mouthfeel. The amount of time the wine is held with the yeast is determined by the winemaker, and many different factors go into his or her decision.

Once the wine has gone through this holding process, the yeast must be extracted from the bottle. Originally the bottles were sealed, not with a cork but with a temporary bottle cap. When it is time to extract the yeast, the bottles are placed, capped ends down, in a shallow freezer. Only the first couple of inches of the wine, where the yeast has settled, are actually frozen. When that part of the liquid is frozen, the yeast freezes into a cube with the liquid. As soon as the bottle is taken from the shallow freezer, it is turned upright and uncapped, and the pressure from the bubbly wine forces the ice, with the frozen yeast, out of the bottle. Before too much of the wine bubbles out, it is placed securely onto a machine with a nozzle that forces what the winemaker calls "dosage" into the wine. Dosage is a small amount of sugar syrup that will finish the wine and adjust the taste—also determined by the winemaker. At that point, the sparkling wine is ready to be corked by

with JOY and LAURENCE STERLING.

another machine and then placed into cases. Sparkling wine does not need to be aged any further, so it is ready to drink.

After my lesson at the winery, Laurence and I met up with Joy and their mother, Audrey Sterling, at her beautiful Victorian house on the vineyard property. Audrey and her husband, Barry Sterling, have not only been growing grapes on this property for years, but they also have an impressive flower, herb, and vegetable garden where they grow lots of the food that they enjoy. Audrey set out a gorgeous spread of fresh fruits and vegetables, as well as cured meats and some fresh goat cheese for us to eat for lunch. Joy opened a selection of their sparkling wines and she led me through a tasting of the food and wine.

Most of us know that Champagne and sparkling wine go very well as an aperitif or with certain fruits and canapés, but I was surprised to find that the wine was perfect with some unexpected things that were on the table. Joy agrees that we should drink what makes us happy. She has been able to throw out conventional thought about what should or shouldn't go together, and therefore has opened herself and others up to some unusual flavor combinations. We tasted foods that I was not expecting to be great with the wine—from the late summer tomatoes and melon to fresh goat cheese— and Joy was able to convince me that sparkling wine really can go with just about anything. More than just for special occasions, sparkling wine can really elevate the flavor of food and add a level of celebration to every experience. A big part of pairing wine with food is the happiness that the experience brings. Learning about sparkling wine, meeting up with my friends the Sterlings, and enjoying the perfect pairings made me very happy indeed.

GARDEN LUNCH by
AUDREY STERLING
of IRON HORSE.

1993 Blanc de Blanc
18 ml BdB LEX
30 ppm SO2

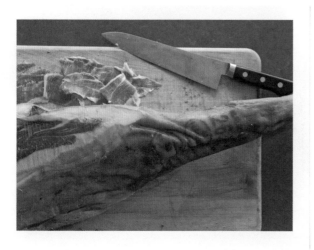

recipes

PERFECT PAIRINGS

SPICY PARMESAN-PISTACHIO CHEESE STRAWS
183

GARLIC-HERBED GOAT CHEESE
182

AVOCADO SALSA VERDE
182

SALMON RILLETTE
181

CARAMELIZED ONION AND GRUYÈRE TART
183

TOMATO BREAD WITH IBÉRICO
185

PEAR AND ENDIVE SALAD
WITH BLUE CHEESE VINAIGRETTE
184

WHOLE ROASTED BEEF TENDERLOIN
WITH RED WINE BUTTER SAUCE
186

ROASTED FINGERLING POTATOES
WITH GARLIC, ROSEMARY AND THYME
186

MACERATED STRAWBERRIES WITH
AGED BALSAMIC ICE CREAM
187

SALMON RILLETTE

Using smoked salmon and poached fresh salmon gives this spread a complex salmon flavor. We serve it as an amuse-bouche at Le Bernardin, but it also makes a perfect appetizer.

SERVES 6

2	*cups dry white wine*
1	*tablespoon minced shallots*
1	*pound fresh boneless skinless salmon fillet, cut into 1-inch pieces*
3	*ounces smoked salmon, diced*
2	*tablespoons thinly sliced fresh chives*
½	*cup mayonnaise*
3	*tablespoons fresh lemon juice*
–	*fine sea salt and freshly ground white pepper*
–	*toasted baguette slices*

Combine the white wine and shallots in a large saucepan and bring to a boil. Simmer over medium-low heat until the shallots are tender, about 2 minutes. Add the salmon pieces and poach until they are just barely opaque, about 2 to 3 minutes. Remove the salmon pieces from the wine and immediately drain them on a baking sheet lined with a towel. Strain the wine, reserving the shallots. Place the salmon and shallots in the refrigerator to cool completely.

Combine the poached salmon pieces, reserved cooked shallots, smoked salmon, chives, and some of the mayonnaise and lemon juice in a stainless steel bowl. Use the mayonnaise and lemon juice sparingly, so that just enough is added to moisten the mixture. Gently stir the mixture until thoroughly combined—do not over-mix or mix too hard. Season the rillette to taste with salt and pepper. Serve cold with toasted baguette slices.

WINE PAIRINGS

The Salmon Rillette recipe is a great dish to serve before a meal as an appetizer or at a cocktail party. Because cocktail parties include many small tastes of things, it is important to serve a very refreshing and food friendly wine to go with a variety of flavors and also to wake up the palate. Both Grüner Veltliner and Sauvignon Blanc are "go to" wines for all-around appeal.

DOMAINE WACHAU GRUNER VELTLINER SMARAGD ACHLEITEN. Wachau, Austria

Grüner Veltliner is the most commonly planted grape variety in Austria and there is where it shows its best results. Additionally, Grüner Veltliner is a great food matching wine and works with almost all types of cuisine. The most famous area for white wine, including Grüner Veltliner, in Austria, the Wachau, is located in the province known as lower Austria. Situated in the Danube River Valley, the Wachau is picturesque with steep hill slopes and vineyards that are set up in terraces.
Award-winning and reliable, Domaine Wachau is classified in single vineyards and produces quite different wines. The single vineyard Achleiten is one of the top vineyards of the region and delivers very mineral driven and focused wines.

DE LADOUCETTE POUILLY-FUMÉ 2007. Loire Valley, France

Sauvignon Blanc from the Loire Valley always delivers very refined and elegant wines. The wines posses a specific tartness that is based on minerality combined with very elegant fruit. Clay and limestone are characteristic components of the soil in this region.
The Commune Pouilly-Fumé is just across of the village Sancerre which is separated by the River Loire. Baron de Ladoucette is the largest and most famous producer in Pouilly-Fumé and has been in family hands between the Comte Lafond and Laoucette families since 1787. No barrels were used to age and store this wine resulting in its crisp and clean characteristics.

GARLIC-HERBED GOAT CHEESE   SERVES 6

Fresh chèvre has a beautiful tart taste. Creamed together with garlic and herbs,
it makes a great spread for slices of crusty bread.

8   *ounces fresh goat cheese*
¼   *cup whole milk*
2   *tablespoons olive oil*
2   *tablespoons chopped fresh thyme leaves*
1   *tablespoon chopped fresh oregano leaves*
1   *tablespoon chopped fresh rosemary leaves*
1   *tablespoon cracked black pepper*
1   *teaspoon finely minced garlic*
–   *fine sea salt*
–   *toasted baguette slices*

Beat the cheese, milk, oil, thyme, oregano, rosemary, pepper and
garlic in a large bowl until well blended and fluffy. Season the
cheese mixture to taste with salt.

Serve at room temperature with toasted baguette slices.

AVOCADO SALSA VERDE   SERVES 6

Ripe avocados are delicious, buttery and slightly nutty. This simple mixture of avocado, lime
juice, jalapeño chili and scallions is a great dip for vegetables and baked tortilla strips, or as
a topping on tacos or salads.

2   *ripe avocados*
1   *jalapeño pepper, stemmed, seeded, and minced*
¼   *cup thinly sliced scallions*
¼   *cup fresh lime juice*
2   *tablespoons chopped fresh cilantro*
2   *tablespoons olive oil*
–   *fine sea salt and freshly ground black pepper*

Cut the avocados in half, remove the pits, and scoop the flesh into
a blender bowl. Add the minced jalapeño pepper, scallions, lime
juice, cilantro and olive oil and blend or pulse until smooth. Season
to taste with salt and pepper and serve with tortilla chips.

*Note: If you prefer more of a chunky texture, mash the avocado in a
mixing bowl and stir in the rest of the ingredients.*

SPICY PARMESAN-PISTACHIO CHEESE STRAWS   SERVES 8

These savory, flaky pastries are so easy to make using frozen puff pastry dough, yet their long, twisted shape makes them an impressive appetizer.

1½ cups grated Parmesan cheese
½ cup chopped toasted pistachios
1 tablespoon freshly ground black pepper
1 teaspoon cayenne pepper
½ teaspoon coarse sea salt
1 package frozen puff pastry dough, thawed
1 large egg, lightly beaten

Stir the Parmesan cheese, pistachios, black pepper, cayenne pepper and salt in a mixing bowl to blend.

Line 2 baking sheets with parchment paper. On a lightly floured work surface, roll out each sheet of puff pastry dough until ⅛-inch thick. Brush the dough with some of the egg and sprinkle evenly with the Parmesan-pistachio mixture. Cut the dough into ⅛-inch-wide strips and transfer the strips to the prepared baking sheets, spacing 1 inch apart. Working with 1 strip at a time, twist each strip to form a spiral. Freeze or refrigerate the strips until they are very cold. Meanwhile, preheat the oven to 450°F.

Bake the cheese straws, rotating halfway through, until they are golden brown, 10 to 12 minutes.

CARAMELIZED ONION AND GRUYÈRE TART   SERVES 6

Gruyère cheese is made in a valley in Switzerland of the same name. It is a great cheese to cook with and has a slightly sweet, nutty flavor. This tart is made by topping puff pastry with caramelized onions and grated Gruyère.

¼ cup olive oil
2 large onions, thinly sliced
2 thyme sprigs
1 small garlic clove, thinly sliced
– fine sea salt and freshly ground black pepper
2 sheets frozen puff pastry dough, thawed and trimmed to six 6-inch rounds
½ cup grated Gruyère cheese

Preheat the oven to 450°F.

Heat the olive oil in a large skillet over medium heat. Add the sliced onions, thyme and garlic. Cook, stirring occasionally, until the onions are soft, about 8 to 10 minutes. Reduce the heat to medium-low and continue cooking, stirring occasionally, for about 30 minutes, or until the onions are well caramelized. Season to taste with salt and pepper.

Line a baking sheet with parchment paper. Place the pastry dough rounds on the baking sheet. Spread the caramelized onions over the pastry rounds, leaving about ½ inch around the edges. Top the onions with the Gruyère cheese. Bake the tarts in the oven for 15 to 20 minutes, or until the crust is golden brown and puffed.

Cut the tarts into wedges and serve warm.

TOMATO BREAD WITH IBÉRICO

It is amazing how much flavor can be imparted by rubbing a slice of toast with a garlic clove and fresh tomato. This simple, classic Spanish snack is topped with the country's famous cured ham.

SERVES 6

¼ loaf crusty bread such as
   a baguette or ciabatta
2 garlic cloves
2 ripe tomatoes, cut in half
½ pound thinly sliced Ibérico ham
   or Serrano ham
– extra virgin olive oil
– coarse sea salt and freshly
   ground black pepper

Cut the loaf of bread crosswise into ½-inch-thick slices. Toast the bread slices until they are golden brown. Lightly rub the toasted bread with the garlic clove, then rub the tomato, cut side down, thoroughly into the toasts. Top the toasts with a couple of slices of Ibérico ham, drizzle the olive oil over the toasts, and season with a few flakes of coarse sea salt and pepper.

PEAR AND ENDIVE SALAD WITH BLUE CHEESE VINAIGRETTE

Greens from the chicory family, like endive, are wonderful when paired with slightly sweet fruit, such as pears. Blue cheese is also a classic companion to pears, making this a great salad of traditionally paired flavors.

SERVES 6-8

¼ cup crumbled blue cheese
3 tablespoons Champagne vinegar
1 tablespoon Dijon mustard
1 tablespoon minced shallot
– fine sea salt and freshly ground
   black pepper
½ cup canola oil
3 small ripe Bartlett pears
3 heads Belgian endive, leaves
   separated, washed and trimmed
1 cup Italian parsley leaves
½ cup toasted walnuts
½ cup crumbled blue cheese (optional)

Whisk ¼ cup of the blue cheese with the Champagne vinegar, Dijon mustard and shallot in a bowl to blend. Season to taste with salt and pepper. Gradually add the canola oil while whisking until emulsified.

Cut the pears in half, then scoop out the cores and slice thinly. Toss the pear slices, endive, parsley and walnuts in a large bowl, and season the salad with salt and pepper. Toss the salad with enough vinaigrette to coat lightly.

Arrange the salad on a large platter and sprinkle with ½ cup of the crumbled blue cheese, if desired.

WHOLE ROASTED BEEF TENDERLOIN
WITH RED WINE BUTTER SAUCE   SERVES 6-8

This is a beautiful recipe to prepare for a special occasion or dinner party. The butter sauce, made with red wine and shallots, is very "old world" but never fails to elevate this exquisite cut of beef.

1   *cup dry red wine*
1   *cup red wine vinegar*
1   *shallot, thinly sliced*
2   *tablespoons whole black peppercorns*
2   *thyme sprigs*
1   *5-pound whole beef tenderloin, trimmed*
–   *fine sea salt and freshly ground black pepper*
3   *tablespoons canola oil*
12 *ounces cold unsalted butter, cut into pieces*

Preheat the oven to 400°F.

Boil the red wine, vinegar, shallot, peppercorns and thyme in a saucepan over high heat until reduced to $\frac{1}{2}$ cup, about 10 minutes. Set the wine reduction aside.

Generously season the tenderloin on all sides with salt and pepper. Heat the oil in a large roasting pan over high heat. Carefully add the tenderloin to the roasting pan, then transfer the pan to the oven and roast the tenderloin, turning every 5 minutes, for 15 to 20 minutes, or until a meat thermometer registers 120°F for medium-rare.

While the tenderloin is roasting, finish the sauce by gradually whisking the cold butter into the warm sauce until it is fully emulsified. Strain the sauce through a fine-mesh sieve into a small saucepan. Season the sauce to taste with salt and pepper; keep warm.

Remove the roasted tenderloin from the oven and let it rest for at least 5 minutes (the meat will continue cooking at this time). Transfer the rested tenderloin to a cutting board and slice it crosswise. Arrange the sliced tenderloin on a large platter. Pour any of the juices from the roasting pan into the butter sauce and serve immediately with the tenderloin.

ROASTED FINGERLING POTATOES
WITH GARLIC, ROSEMARY AND THYME   SERVES 8

Fingerling potatoes are beautiful, small tubers that come in a variety of colors and possess a very concentrated potato flavor. They are best when cut in half and simply tossed with oil, garlic and herbs, then roasted in the oven.

186

3   *pounds fingerling potatoes, washed*
2   *garlic heads, cloves separated*
¼   *cup olive oil*
–   *fine sea salt and freshly ground black pepper*
4   *rosemary sprigs*
4   *thyme sprigs*
3   *tablespoons unsalted butter*

Preheat the oven to 400°F.

Cut the fingerling potatoes in half and place them on a large baking sheet with the garlic cloves. Drizzle the olive oil over the potatoes and garlic and season with salt and pepper. Add the rosemary and thyme sprigs and roast until the potatoes are golden brown and tender, 20 to 25 minutes.

Remove the pan from the oven and toss the potatoes with butter. Serve hot.

MACERATED STRAWBERRIES
WITH AGED BALSAMIC ICE CREAM   SERVES 4

Accenting strawberries with balsamic vinegar makes for a classic pairing. The strawberries here are simply prepared to form a light syrup that's spooned over a refreshing balsamic ice cream. Although a little balsamic vinegar goes a long way, the success of the ice cream depends heavily on its quality.

ICE CREAM

- 1 *pint whole milk*
- 1 *tablespoon nonfat dry milk powder*
- 10 *tablespoons granulated sugar*
- 4 *large egg yolks*
- ½ *cup heavy cream*
- 2 *tablespoons fine-quality aged balsamic vinegar (see note)*

STRAWBERRIES

- 2 *pints fresh strawberries, rinsed, hulled, and quartered lengthwise*
- 2 *tablespoons granulated sugar*
- 1 *lemon, zest grated, juiced*
- 2-3 *basil leaves, coarsely chopped*

Place the milk in a saucepan and whisk in the dry milk powder to rehydrate. Gently bring to a boil. Whisk the sugar and egg yolks in a large bowl to blend. Gradually whisk the hot milk mixture into the yolk mixture, a little at a time, so as not to curdle the yolks. Return the mixture to the saucepan and stir over low heat until slightly thickened, about 6 to 8 minutes. Remove from the heat and whisk in the heavy cream and balsamic vinegar. Cover and refrigerate the custard for at least 12 hours to allow it to mature.

Process the custard in an ice cream machine according to the manufacturer's instructions. Transfer the ice cream to a container, then cover and allow it to harden in the freezer.

Toss the strawberries, sugar, lemon juice and zest, and basil in a large bowl. Cover and let stand at room temperature for about 2 hours to macerate. Cover and refrigerate until well-chilled.

Serve the ice cream with macerated strawberries.

Note: You may substitute regular balsamic vinegar for the aged balsamic vinegar. To substitute, simmer the regular balsamic vinegar in a saucepan until it is thick enough to coat the back of a spoon, then allow it to cool completely (it will continue to thicken as it cools).

187

Chapter 9

OIL AND WINE

Fonterutoli, Italy

OLIVE OIL TASTING at LE BERNARDIN.

CREATING A GREAT DISH MEANS THAT EVERY INGREDIENT MUST BE THE VERY BEST THAT CAN BE FOUND. At Le Bernardin, we spend lots of time tasting and considering various flavors and products. Olive oil is an ingredient that we use in many dishes and in many different ways. It is very much like wine, in that it can take on various characteristics dictated by a variety of factors. Geography, varietals, vintage, craftsmanship, storage and the weather are a few of the variables. Because of this, we can't rely on the same brand of olive oil to taste the same year after year.

A couple of times a year, we gather the chefs together for an oil tasting. We pour five or six different oils into numbered bowls so that no one can make a judgment based on brand loyalty or any other prejudice. We all take tastes, discuss what we like and don't like, and then narrow it down to about three choices. Then we taste through those three again and consider how the oils might blend with and highlight our food rather than overpower it or change it too drastically. We also taste the oils with some of our food because, even though we might like the oil on its own, it might not be right with the type of food we make. Typically, we are looking for oil that has a more delicate flavor— a bit lighter so that the oil enhances the fish that we serve, but doesn't cover up the flavor of the dish itself. It is always interesting to unveil the olive oil that we end up choosing as our favorite. Sometimes it is a brand that we have never used at the restaurant before. This past year, the winner was oil that we've used in the past, abandoned for a little while because the flavor profile had changed, and now we have come back to using it again. The decision reinforced the importance of tasting every ingredient often and with an open mind.

Traveling through Italy, and exploring the very famous wine region of Chianti, I was constantly reminded of olive oil because of the olive groves everywhere. Looking across the landscape of Tuscany, the distant textures look like patches

of lines and dots. The dots are the olive orchards and the lines are grapevine rows. It's a scene that looks like a fairytale illustration, and seeing it in person caused me to wonder about the history and process of both the wine and the oil production. Filippo Mazzei, whose family has lived and worked in Chianti since 1435, invited me to come and tour Castello di Fonterutoli—his family's home, winery and olive oil production facility. The charming, old world town is ancient with Roman roads winding around the beautiful homes, businesses and churches and into the piazza. The scene is striking and a little surreal—it truly feels like a step into the past.

Pressing olives for oil is an ancient practice and has been very important for the economy and livelihood of people not just in Italy, but all over Mediterranean Europe. Also, it changed the way people ate. The oil altered cooking techniques and changed the flavors of the food and, ultimately, the palates of the people. Filippo showed me his family's ancient wine cellars and the place where the giant terracotta oil jugs were kept and still remain, although not used. The jugs are about four feet high and three feet around with heavy wooden lids to cover them. Filippo explained that after the olive oil was pressed, it was put into these jugs and kept in the cellars for storage. People who wanted to buy the oil would bring their own containers and ladle just enough oil to last two or three weeks. While the jugs are very beautiful, they were not the perfect vessels for storing the oil, as using them made it difficult to keep the oil very clean and exposed the oil to a lot of oxygen, which expedites the decline of its quality.

The trees are beautiful—sturdy, gnarled trunks branching out with slender, silvery leaves and bearing the small, hard olive fruit. The fruit starts out green and then turns a deep purple-black color. If you pick an olive to eat it

CHOOSING OLIVE OIL

Different olive oils are good for different things. There is no need to spend lots of money on very fine estate olive oil if you are only going to cook with it or fry something in it. Even though olive oil can be a good oil to use for cooking, I don't always cook with it because it changes the way food tastes during that stage and has a tendency to impart a little too much flavor. So when I want a milder flavor, I use canola oil for cooking instead. If you are drizzling it over good food, however, a great olive oil can open up a window of flavor to that food and has the potential to vastly improve a dish.

Extra virgin indicates oil that has been extracted from the first pressing of the olives and technically refers to an acid level that is in the oil. The oil and juice of the olive, extracted during the first pressing, have very little free oleic acid, and are generally better than oil extracted from later pressings.

Cold-pressed olive oil means that the pressing apparatus does not add or create heat. The addition of heat by friction or machinery will lower the quality of the oil.

Tasting olive oil is the real way to choose what you like. Olive oil comes from different regions and different landscapes, and therefore—just like wine—takes on the taste of terroir.

Enjoy exploring different oils and the various flavors that olive oil provides.

FONTERUTOLI, ITALY.

straight from the tree, you immediately want to spit it out—it's very bitter, even when perfectly ripe. Somewhere down the line, people discovered that you could extract rich oil from the fruit and cure the hard olives in brine to make them edible. It takes a lot of work, but the flavors coaxed out of this bitter fruit are subtle and complex. Olive trees thrive in the same environmental conditions as some of the great wines of the world, and those elements also give olive oil its complex flavors. Two factors that are important for growing olives are orientation to the sunlight and elevation. Cool evenings and hot days produce the most flavorful olives—just like the conditions that are perfect for growing grapes. It was starting to be clear to me that olives and grapes have lots of similarities. Usually, olives are ready for harvesting in late autumn, and in this part of Tuscany the harvest takes place in late October through mid-November.

Filippo then took me to an olive orchard that was located just next to the pressing facility—a state-of-the-art operation set in the heart of the orchards. Here, the olives were perfect for harvesting, having turned from green to black. He encouraged me to pick an olive and press it into my hand. Without too much pressure, the olive broke open and dripped rich oil into my palm. The oil that came out of the olive was slick and very smooth.

Once the olives are ready to harvest, it usually means that every worker heads into the orchards to do the work. On small family estates, friends, relatives, and even townspeople will gather in the orchard to help. Many growers still pick olives by hand but there are some machines that can help as well. To begin the harvest, huge pieces of burlap are spread out under the trees. The harvesters use the burlap sheets to catch the olives as they are shaken off the tree by a special mechanical rake that gently vibrates the branches. The rakes do a very good job of extracting the olives from the branches without harming the tree. I was allowed to help work with the shaking machine for a bit, and while the machine worked quickly and efficiently, it was heavy and must be held up and moved around in the trees; so I learned pretty early into the task that it is hard work.

GATHERING OLIVES to MAKE OLIVE OIL.

Once collected, the olives are taken to the pressing facility where they are washed very well and separated from the leaves. They go through a machine that cuts the fruit so that the oil will come out easily when the pressing begins. These machines work fast and at a certain temperature so that little damage is done to the fruit before the oil is extracted. Then the olives go into a big tank room where the oil is pressed out and sent through filters and on to the holding tanks. In between the pressing and filtration it is possible to taste the oil. The unfiltered olive oil is very fresh and bright, and you can really get a glimpse into what the oil might taste like at the end. Once filtered and put into tanks (according to batches), the tasting of each oil begins. This part is very similar to the process of tasting and blending wine. The oils at this point are clear and bright green in color, and I was stunned by the difference between the filtered and the unfiltered oil. The result is a very round, clean flavor that makes it possible to really understand the complex flavor profiles. While these individual oils are very good, the process goes on to blending, where each oil is tasted and then blended by a master to get the very best flavor for bottling that year. While there is a lot of science behind this process, Filippo Mazzei explained that there is also an important "human side" to the process of "understanding the flavor and nuance of each harvest." I totally agree, and witnessing the job of making the oil has changed the way I will taste olive oil forever.

THE HILLS, OLIVE GROVES and VINEYARDS of CHIANTI.

with FILIPPO MAZZEI at CASTELLO DI FONTERUTOLI.

recipes

OIL AND WINE

WHITE WINE–CITRUS SPRITZERS
211

PORTOBELLO "FRIES"
WITH TRUFFLED AÏOLI
205

SPICED OLIVES
204

GREEN OLIVE TAPENADE
204

GRAPE, ALMOND, AND
RADICCHIO SALAD WITH BLACK OLIVES
207

SNAPPER TARTARE
WITH OLIVES, LEMON AND FENNEL
209

SEARED SKIRT STEAK AND SPINACH SALAD
WITH RED WINE-SHALLOT VINAIGRETTE
207

CHICKEN PAILLARD
WITH TOMATOES, FENNEL AND OLIVES
203

PAN-ROASTED ARCTIC CHAR
OVER BLACK OLIVE POTATOES
AND MELTED CHERRY TOMATOES
210

PAIN AU CHOCOLAT
211

CHICKEN PAILLARD WITH TOMATOES, FENNEL AND OLIVES

The inspiration for this chicken paillard recipe came after a visit to the olive orchards of Castello di Fonterutoli in Chianti, Italy. Topped with tomatoes, herbs, fennel, pine nuts and capers, it is reflective of the kinds of ingredients commonly found in that region of Italy.

SERVES 4

- 1 *cup diced seeded peeled tomatoes*
- ¾ *cup thinly sliced fennel*
- ½ *cup green olives, pitted and sliced*
- ½ *cup minced shallots*
- ¼ *cup pine nuts, toasted*
- ¼ *cup raisins, plumped in dry white wine*
- 2 *tablespoons capers*
- 4 *thyme sprigs, leaves removed*
- 2 *garlic cloves, minced*
- ½ *cup olive oil, divided*
- – *fine sea salt and freshly ground black pepper*
- 4 *skinless boneless chicken breasts, butterflied and lightly pounded flat*
- 3 *tablespoons fresh basil chiffonade*
- 2 *tablespoons chopped fresh Italian parsley*

Preheat the oven to 450°F.

Toss the tomatoes, fennel, green olives, shallots, pine nuts, raisins, capers, thyme leaves and garlic in a mixing bowl. Drizzle most of the olive oil over the vegetables and season to taste with salt and pepper.

Season the chicken breasts on both sides with salt and pepper. Place the chicken in a single layer on a large baking dish. Cover the chicken with the tomato mixture and drizzle the remaining olive oil over and around the chicken. Bake for 15 to 20 minutes, or until the chicken is cooked through. Sprinkle the basil and parsley over the chicken and serve immediately.

WINE PAIRINGS

The flavors of the Mediterranean always seem rich and sophisticated even though usually the preparation required to execute a dish with these flavors is minimal. Bold flavors like fennel and basil and the acidity of tomatoes and capers can be challenging to pair with wine, but keep in mind that the regions that celebrate the flavors in these recipes are some of the greatest wine-growing areas in the world.

ARGIOLAS COSTAMOLINO VERMENTINO 2008. Sardinia, Italy

Vermentino is an aromatic white grape variety mostly planted in Sardinia. Costamolino is a refreshing wine that is very well structured and has its typical exotic fruit flavors characterizing the variety. The Argiolas Winery was established in 1937 and currently has 625 acres under vine, focusing on the typical, indigenous varietals of Sardinia like Cannonau, Monica, Nuragus and Vermentino. Not just a beautiful island for a vacation, Sardinia produces wines looking to be discovered, and they deserve attention. Vermentino is especially nice with Mediterranean dishes, where olives and tomatoes are very often used.

J. ALBERTO SINGLE VINEYARD MALBEC, BODEGA NOEMIA 2009. Patagonia, Argentina

For the last couple of years, Argentina has had big success with its major red varietal, Malbec. Very popular in the last century in Bordeaux, Malbec still gives the backbone in the French AOC Cahors. Malbec is the leading grape varietal in most of the wine growing regions of Argentina and is often blended with Bordeaux varietals such as Cabernet Sauvignon and Merlot. Mendoza, the largest region in Argentina, delivers quite powerful and rich styles of Malbec.
Bodega Noemia, located in the Rio Negro region of southern Patagonia is certainly considered one of the best wineries in Argentina. The old vine vineyards that they own always deliver rich and complex wines with great structure. Patagonian Malbecs tend to have more red fruit characteristics and are a little softer in tannins than their firmer counterparts from Mendoza. This wine is rich but very drinkable.

SPICED OLIVES   MAKES 2 CUPS

It's easy to add flavor to regular cured olives and, once mixed, the olives will continue
to take on stronger flavors as they marinate.

2   *cups mixed olives, such as picholine,*
Cerignola, Niçoise, Gaeta, or Kalamata
¼   *cup olive oil*
1   *lemon, zested and juiced*
1   *garlic clove, thinly sliced*
1   *teaspoon freshly ground black pepper*
1   *teaspoon ground cumin*
1   *teaspoon toasted fennel seeds*
½   *teaspoon dried hot red chili flakes*

Combine all of the ingredients in a bowl and mix well. Let the
olives marinate at room temperature for at least 1 hour before
serving. The marinated olives can be refrigerated, covered, for
up to 2 weeks.

GREEN OLIVE TAPENADE   MAKES 1 CUP

Tapenade is a chopped olive mixture from the Provence region of France. This one is very basic
and easy to prepare from things that most of us have in the pantry. Capers, herbs and mustard
mix with the olives to make a wonderful spread for bread or crackers.

1½   *cups green olives such as picholine*
or nafplion, pitted
¼   *cup drained capers*
¼   *cup olive oil*
2   *tablespoons fresh lemon juice*
1   *tablespoon Dijon mustard*
1   *teaspoon fresh thyme leaves*
1   *garlic clove, chopped*
–   *crusty bread or toasted bread*

Place all of the ingredients, except the bread, in a food processor
bowl and pulse until well blended.

Serve the tapenade with crusty bread or toast.

PORTOBELLO "FRIES" WITH TRUFFLED AÏOLI   SERVES 4

Thick strips of portobello mushrooms are breaded and fried to create a flavorful
alternative to potato fries.

TRUFFLE AÏOLI

  2   *large egg yolks*
  2   *tablespoons fresh lemon juice*
  1   *teaspoon minced garlic*
  ½   *cup canola oil*
  ½   *cup olive oil*
  2   *tablespoons white truffle oil, approx.*
  –   *fine sea salt and freshly ground
        white pepper*

PORTOBELLO "FRIES"

  4   *portobello mushrooms*
1½   *cups fine dried bread crumbs*
  ½   *cup grated Pecorino Romano cheese*
  1   *teaspoon freshly ground black pepper*
  ¾   *teaspoon fine sea salt*
  ½   *teaspoon dried thyme*
  ¼   *cup all purpose flour*
  2   *large eggs, lightly beaten*
  –   *canola oil for frying*

Combine the yolks, lemon juice and garlic in a blender. With the blender
on medium speed, drizzle the canola oil and olive oil into the yolk
mixture in a slow steady stream until the aïoli is emulsified and well
blended. Season with the truffle oil, salt and pepper. Transfer the aïoli to
a small bowl and set aside.

Trim the stems from the mushrooms, scrape out the gills, and gently
wipe the mushroom caps with a damp cloth. Cut the mushroom caps
into ½-inch-wide strips.

Combine the bread crumbs, cheese, pepper, salt and thyme in a shallow
dish. Place the flour and eggs in separate shallow dishes. Toss the mushroom strips in the flour to coat evenly, then dip them into the eggs and
roll them in the bread crumb mixture.

Heat about 1 inch of oil in a large skillet over medium heat. Working in
batches, place the breaded mushroom strips in the hot oil and cook on
all sides until golden brown, 3 to 4 minutes. Transfer to a tray lined with
paper towels. Serve hot with the aïoli.

205

GRAPE, ALMOND AND RADICCHIO SALAD WITH BLACK OLIVES

Radicchio is part of the chicory family and has beautiful burgundy-colored leaves with white ribs. The flavor is pleasantly bitter, working very well with the sweet grapes and brined olives.

SERVES 4

- 1 *head radicchio, cut into bite-size pieces*
- 1 *head Belgian endive, cut into bite-size pieces*
- ½ *cup black olives, thinly sliced*
- ½ *cup green grapes, cut in half*
- ½ *cup whole almonds, toasted and lightly chopped*
- 2 *tablespoons white balsamic vinegar*
- ¼ *cup olive oil*
- – *fine sea salt and freshly ground black pepper*

Place the radicchio and endive in a large bowl and add the black olives, grapes and almonds. Dress the salad with the balsamic vinegar and olive oil and season with salt and pepper. Toss to coat and serve immediately.

SEARED SKIRT STEAK AND SPINACH SALAD WITH RED WINE-SHALLOT VINAIGRETTE

A quick, hot searing is the perfect way to cook this cut of steak. Slicing the meat thinly and laying the strips across a bed of spinach with a shallot vinaigrette makes this a wonderful main dish salad.

SERVES 4

- 2 *cups dry red wine*
- 2 *shallots, finely diced*
- 2 *Italian parsley sprigs*
- 2 *thyme sprigs*
- 1 *teaspoon cracked black peppercorns*
- – *fine sea salt and freshly ground black pepper*
- 2 *tablespoons red wine vinegar*
- ½ *cup extra virgin olive oil*
- 2 *tablespoons canola oil*
- 1½ *pounds skirt steak, trimmed to four 6-inch steaks*
- 3 *cups fresh baby spinach*
- 4 *large white button mushrooms, cleaned and thinly sliced*

Combine the red wine, shallots and parsley in a nonreactive saucepan and simmer over medium-high heat until reduced to 0 cup. Remove the saucepan from the heat and discard the parsley and thyme sprigs. Add the cracked pepper, season to taste with salt, and whisk in the red wine vinegar and olive oil. Set aside.

Heat the canola oil in a large heavy stainless steel or cast-iron skillet over high heat. Generously season the skirt steaks with salt and freshly ground pepper. Carefully add the seasoned steaks to the pan, making sure not to crowd the pan, and sear until evenly crusted, 2 to 3 minutes per side for medium-rare. Transfer the cooked steaks to a cutting board, wipe out the pan, and repeat, if necessary, with the remaining steaks. Let the steaks rest for at least 5 minutes. Gently warm the red wine vinaigrette in the same pan over low heat.

While the steaks are resting, combine the spinach and mushrooms in a bowl, season to taste with salt and pepper, and lightly dress with the warm vinaigrette. Divide the salad on 4 plates. Slice the steaks against the grain and place the slices on top of each salad. Spoon more of the vinaigrette over and around the salad and serve immediately.

207

SNAPPER TARTARE WITH OLIVES, LEMON AND FENNEL

Many people are accustomed to tuna tartare, but snapper has a wonderful flavor and texture that is beautiful with olives, fennel and lemon.

SERVES 4

9   *ounces red snapper fillet, cut to small dice*
2   *tablespoons extra virgin olive oil*
1   *tablespoon chopped green olives*
    (such as picholine olives)
1   *tablespoon lemon oil*
1   *teaspoon lemon confit, blanched and*
    julienned (see note)
–   *fine sea salt and freshly ground white pepper*
2   *tablespoons julienned fresh mint*
2   *baby fennel, shaved and crisped in ice water*
1   *lemon, cut in half*

LEMON CONFIT

6   *lemons, scrubbed*
3   *cups kosher salt*
–   *1-quart canning jar with a tight-fitting lid,*
    sterilized in boiling water

Stir together the snapper, olive oil, green olives, lemon oil and lemon confit in a bowl. Season to taste with salt and pepper.

Place a 3½-inch ring mold in the center of 1 plate and loosely pack about 4 tablespoons of the tartar into the ring mold, then lift off the ring. Repeat on 3 more plates with the remaining tartare. Top the tartare with mint and shaved fennel. Squeeze the lemon juice over the fish and serve immediately.

For the Lemon Confit: Quarter each lemon lengthwise, starting at one end and keeping the other end attached. Pour a layer of salt into the bottom of the jar. Heavily salt each of the lemons inside and out and pack them into the jar, using all of the salt between the layers and pushing down to release the juices. Seal the jar and refrigerate.

Let the lemons cure for at least 1 month before using.

To use the confit, separate the lemon quarters, cut away all the flesh from the rind and discard the flesh. Rinse or blanch the lemon rind before use.

Note: Lemon confit, also known as preserved lemon, can be found in most gourmet markets, but it's very easy to make a batch at home and kept refrigerated for up to a year.

PAN-ROASTED ARCTIC CHAR OVER BLACK OLIVE POTATOES AND MELTED CHERRY TOMATOES   SERVES 4

Arctic char is a delicious fish that comes from icy waters. Its flavor and texture are a cross between that of salmon and trout. The melted tomatoes retain their tanginess but caramelize while cooking.

3   *medium Yukon Gold potatoes*

6   *tablespoons plus ¼ cup extra virgin olive oil*

1   *shallot, thinly sliced*

1   *garlic clove, thinly sliced*

1   *pint cherry tomatoes, cut in half*

–   *fine sea salt and freshly ground white pepper*

3   *tablespoons red wine vinegar*

¼   *cup Niçoise olives, pitted and chopped*

2   *tablespoons canola oil*

4   *(6-ounce) arctic char fillets*

3   *tablespoons chopped fresh Italian parsley*

Place the potatoes in a small pot of cold salted water and cook over medium heat until they are tender, 20 to 25 minutes.

While the potatoes are cooking, heat 6 tablespoons of the olive oil in a large saucepan over medium heat, then add the shallots and garlic and sauté for 3 minutes. Add the cherry tomatoes, season with salt and pepper, and cook until they are melted and the shallots and garlic start to caramelize, about 10 minutes. Remove the pan from the heat and add the red wine vinegar.

When the potatoes are tender, drain them and allow them to cool enough to be handled. Peel the potatoes and crush them with a fork. Pour the remaining ¼ cup of olive oil over the potatoes, add the chopped olives, and season to taste with salt and pepper. Keep warm.

For the arctic char, divide the canola oil between 2 sauté pans and heat the oil over high heat until it is very hot but not smoking. Season the arctic char on both sides with salt and pepper. Gently place 2 fillets in each pan and sear the fish until golden brown and crisp, 3 to 5 minutes. Turn the fish over and finish cooking for 3 to 5 minutes, or until a metal skewer can be easily inserted into the fish and, when left in for 5 seconds, feels just warm when touched to the lip.

While the fish is cooking, bring the cherry tomato sauce to a simmer and add the chopped parsley. To serve, place the mashed potatoes in the center of each of 4 plates. Place the arctic char on top of the potatoes and spoon the tomato sauce around the potatoes on each plate. Serve immediately.

PAIN AU CHOCOLAT   SERVES 4

This dessert is inspired by the classic pastry of buttery croissant dough encasing a bar of soft chocolate. Here we play off the idea of bread and chocolate, while also highlighting the combination's affinity for olive oil.

½ cup whole milk
¼ cup granulated sugar
2 large egg yolks
6 ounces fine-quality bittersweet chocolate, coarsely chopped
¾ cup heavy cream, cold
1 baguette
– extra virgin olive oil, as needed
– coarse sea salt

Place the milk in a small saucepan and gently bring to a boil. Meanwhile, whisk the sugar and eggs yolks in a bowl to blend. Very slowly whisk the milk into the egg yolk mixture. Pour the egg mixture back into the saucepan and return to low heat. Continue to cook, stirring continuously, until the mixture thickens slightly, about 10 minutes. Remove from the heat.

Place the chopped chocolate in a clean bowl and whisk in the hot milk mixture, a small amount at a time, stirring to blend. After all the milk has been incorporated, cover the chocolate mixture and cool to room temperature.

In another bowl, vigorously whip the heavy cream until it begins to hold its form and soft peaks develop. Fold the whipped cream into the cooled chocolate mixture and divide the chocolate mousse among 4 serving vessels. Refrigerate for 1 hour before serving.

Preheat the oven to 325°F. Cut some of the baguette as thinly as possible into 8 thin slices; reserve the remaining baguette for another use. Arrange the baguette slices on a baking sheet and drizzle lightly with olive oil. Toast the slices in the oven for 5 to 10 minutes, or until crisp and lightly browned.

To serve, place the toasts on top of the chocolate mousse dishes, drizzle the olive oil over and around the mousse, and top with a pinch of sea salt.

WHITE WINE–CITRUS SPRITZERS   MAKES 4 COCKTAILS

This refreshing drink is just right for a cocktail party. It uses the Italian aperitivo, *Aperol* (which is a bit like Campari), lemon and white wine.

LEMON SYRUP

2 lemons
½ cup sugar

SPRITZERS

– ice cubes
8 ounces dry white wine
4 ounces Aperol
– seltzer water
4 orange peel twists

Using a vegetable peeler, remove the yellow peel from the lemons, avoiding the white pith under the peel. Squeeze the lemon juice into a small saucepan. Add the lemon peels and sugar to the lemon juice and simmer, while stirring, until all of the sugar has dissolved. Strain through a fine-mesh sieve and let cool.

For each spritzer: Fill a tall Collins glass with ice and stir in 2 ounces of the white wine, 1 ounce of the Aperol and 1 ounce of the lemon syrup. Top with a splash of seltzer water and garnish with an orange twist.

211

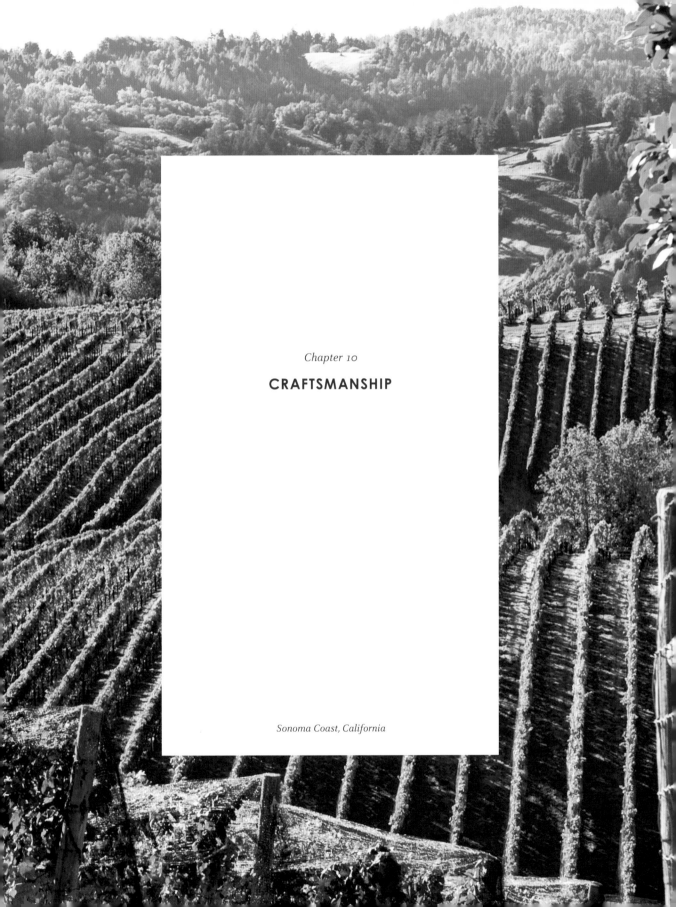

Chapter 10

CRAFTSMANSHIP

Sonoma Coast, California

JUSTO THOMAS, Le Bernardin.

TRUE CRAFTSMANSHIP—TO BE THE MASTER OF A SET OF SKILLS—TAKES YEARS OF STUDY AND PRACTICE. Researching and reading about a skill can be important, but the "craft" of something comes when physical artistry is set in motion. Culinary professionals, including chefs and winemakers, can certainly be considered craftsmen, but there are others in the kitchen whom I also consider craftsmen—truly skilled and talented individuals who have worked hard to get to their current level of expertise.

Justo Thomas is the butcher of all of the fish that we use at Le Bernardin. Very early in the morning, deliveries of fresh fish start coming in. Immediately, Justo checks them to make sure they are perfect and then begins cutting them up for our lunch and dinner service that day. Each type of fish is different so the same butchering technique cannot be used on every fish. Justo enjoys his job and is a true master craftsman. I've never seen anyone work faster than him at this task. He works very quickly but precisely, leaving no wasted product. When he goes on vacation it takes three people twice as long to do what he accomplishes by 2:00 p.m. each day. Justo has a lot of respect for the fish too, and it is always impressive to watch him work. Once he has cleaned and scaled the fish and made the initial cuts, it is also his job to cut the fish into the exact portions that we use on the line in the kitchen. Consistent portions are very important because we want every plate to look exactly the same and we want to make sure the customers are being served what they expect. Justo has a little scale to weigh the fish at his station, but he knows the fish and his craft so well that he instinctively knows how much he is cutting, and really doesn't even need a scale. I think he only uses it to double check his work as sort of a little challenge to himself to keep on top of his game. Since the orders come in so fast during service, the line cooks must have each piece of fish in perfect condition and ready to be cooked. The care that Justo takes makes the chef's job easier and they can concentrate on cooking the fish perfectly.

There are many other kinds of craftsmen in the culinary industry, and I imagine that some of the most intense jobs are those in the wine industry. Opening a bottle of wine, pouring it into a glass, and enjoying that wine is something that most of us take for granted. There are so many factors that go into each

grape, each fermentation tank, each barrel, bottle and glass—it's mind-blowing really. Working with wine requires more than just practicing one thing over and over, because the variables change constantly.

It is no secret that making great wine requires an enormous amount of work and hinges on factors that are not always in our control. Growing grapes is where the process starts. From the technicalities of soil management, to the proper harvesting, all the way to putting wine into barrels for aging and then eventually into bottles for selling, the entire process requires true craftsmanship and artistry. My friends at Flowers Vineyard and Winery, on the Sonoma Coast of California, invited me to witness the process. I found out that there is so much more than I thought to the task of getting a good bottle of wine to the table.

For a vineyard manager, the labor of keeping grapevines healthy is a year-round effort. Soil management, pruning, and keeping pests away are just some of the work that goes into producing beautiful grapes. Flowers' position on the Sonoma Coast is very special and provides the perfect cool nights and hot days that grapes love, as well as some gusts of sea breezes that provide flavor in a very good way. All of these things make up the *terroir* that will give identity to the wine. Once the grapes are perfectly ripe (the winemaker will test the grapes over a few days to check for taste and sugar content) the harvest team comes in to start picking the fruit. The work is very physical because the workers have to bend over to get to all of the grape clusters, the sun is extremely hot, and the bins of grapes that they carry through the rows of vines are heavy. The harvest team works very quickly because once the grapes have hit their peak, the fruit must be picked immediately.

STEMWARE AND DECANTERS

Tasting wine properly, especially when doing something technical like blending, is very important. While most of us are not wine professionals, it is still very nice to use the right tools for serving and tasting wine.
Stemware that is fashioned into a specific shape for tasting a specific varietal may seem a bit extravagant, but there is definitely a difference in how a wine will change once it is exposed to oxygen when it is poured. You don't need to buy different stems for each and every kind of wine, but it is nice to have a set of red and white wineglasses. Red wineglasses will be a bit larger than white wineglasses; the size and shape relate to how oxygen affects the different wines. Red wines generally need to have a bit more exposure to air in order to open up. Quality stemware also has very thin crystal or glass bowls and rims. Not only does it make for a more elegant glass, but the various shapes of glasses help the wine hit certain parts of the tongue first. It can also be helpful to buy at least one decanter. Older wines benefit from decanting because they need to be opened at least 30 minutes before drinking and be exposed to more air than is provided by just opening the bottle. The act of pouring wine from a bottle into a decanter before it is served introduces more oxygen that will help the wine to open up. Also, older wines,

FLOWERS VINEYARD
SONOMA, California.

as well as unfiltered wines, will have some sediment that has settled in the bottom of the bottle. This is normal, and utilizing a decanter will allow a host or server to pour all but the last inch or so of wine into the decanter, ensuring that the least amount of sediment will make its way into the glass. A decanter can also help if you have opened up a wine that seems very green or tight. Again, the introduction of more oxygen can only help.

From harvest, the grapes go through a sorting process where workers view every cluster to pick out any fruit that might have mold or damage. Next, the grapes are put into huge tanks to begin the fermentation process. Over the course of a few days, the grapes will begin to break down, releasing their juices and developing complex flavors. During this time, the winemaker will "punch down" or stir up the juice with the grape skins and seeds so that the flavors will continue to evolve. Keeping the skins and seeds with the juice for a while develops color, flavor and tannins in the wine. The juice will also go through an aeration process that incorporates oxygen into the tank, giving more power to the yeasts that are working inside the wine. At these various points, the winemaker will continue to taste the wine. It is very new and a little bit viscous at this time, but there are already some nice characteristics developing and the winemaker can get an idea of what is happening. After several days, the juice is finally separated from the solids and drained into new oak barrels from the Burgundy region of France, where it will stay for whatever length of time the winemaker feels is necessary. He will use what is called a "thief" (a long glass cylinder) to take a little of the wine out of the barrel to taste it at different intervals. Once he feels it is ready, the wine will either be put straight into bottles for selling or it will go through the blending process.

The process of blending wine is really an art form in itself. Sometimes winemakers will blend different varietals together, and sometimes they will put together the same kind of grape (usually all from the same vintage) to get a certain taste and structure that makes the wine even better. At the Flowers Winery, I was invited to sit in on a blending session to make a Pinot Noir *cuvée* (the French word for "blend"). We started with a core wine that was from a certain block (a particular section of the vineyard) of grapes. We also had four or five other Pinot Noirs to begin testing with the core. It is amazing that some people are so good at blending, because it really uses all of your senses. Obviously, smell and taste are key factors here, but also the texture of a wine, or how it feels in your mouth, is important. Color can also be a deciding factor because we are all influenced visually. There are no right or wrong answers when blending wine once you have started with a good product. After that, it is a little bit of science, a little bit of instinct, some skill for sure, and in the end it is art. Taking little amounts of this and that wine, writing down each measurement, tasting and consideration is fun to do—it is a lot like cooking—but to make it an occupation and to do it well, with soul and skill, is true craftsmanship.

TOM HINDE walks me through the BLENDING PROCESS.

219

The HARVEST CREW and STAFF at FLOWERS.

JOAN and WALT FLOWERS.

TOM HINDE and KEIKO NICCOLINI.

BARELY-COOKED SCALLOPS WITH TOMATO COMPOTE
AND CHAMPAGNE BEURRE BLANC SERVES 4 AS AN APPETIZER

The scallops in this recipe are cut crosswise into thin slices, then barely cooked. They are served with a classic butter sauce made with Champagne instead of the traditional white wine, resulting in a very elegant dish.

TOMATO COMPOTE

2	*tablespoons olive oil*
½	*cup diced shallots*
1	*teaspoon minced garlic*
2	*cups peeled, seeded, and diced tomatoes*
1	*tablespoon tomato paste*
–	*fine sea salt, freshly ground black pepper*

CHAMPAGNE BEURRE BLANC

1	*cup Champagne or other dry sparkling wine*
¼	*cup finely minced shallots*
½	*cup unsalted butter (8 tablespoons)*
–	*fine sea salt, freshly ground black pepper*

SCALLOPS

¾	*pound diver scallops*
1	*tablespoon olive oil*
–	*fine sea salt, freshly ground white pepper*
2	*tablespoons thinly sliced fresh chives*

Preheat the oven to 400°F.

Heat the olive oil in a heavy sauté pan over medium heat. Add the shallots and garlic and cook until soft, about 5 minutes. Add the tomatoes and tomato paste and cook over medium-low heat, stirring frequently, until almost dry, about 15 minutes. Season the compote to taste with salt and pepper. Remove from the heat and cover to keep warm.

Combine the Champagne and shallots in a small saucepan and boil over medium-high heat until reduced to ¼ cup, about 10 minutes. The reduction can be made ahead and kept covered. To finish the beurre blanc sauce, whisk in the butter 1 tablespoon at a time until fully blended. Season the sauce to taste with salt and pepper.

Slice the scallops crosswise into ½-inch-thick slices. Lay the scallop slices in a single layer on a baking sheet. Drizzle the olive oil over the scallops and season with salt and pepper. Place the pan in the oven and roast the scallops until they are just warm to the touch, about 4 minutes. Remove the scallops from the oven.

Set a ring mold in the center of 1 plate and spoon some of the tomato compote in the ring mold. Lift the ring and repeat on 3 more plates with the remaining tomato compote. Arrange the scallops in a pinwheel pattern over the compote. Sprinkle the chives on top of the scallops, spoon the sauce over, and serve immediately.

WINE PAIRINGS

Barely-cooked scallops with a tomato compote and champagne beurre blanc paired with either a white Burgundy from the Meursault or the Spanish Albariño make elegant combinations that are just as comfortable on a white tablecloth in a formal dining room as they are on an outdoor table for two on a spring night.

DOMAINE PIERRE MATROT MEURSAULT 2007.
Burgundy, France

In Meursault, a large village in the Côte de Beaune district of Burgundy, the cellars are based deeper in the soil, which enables many growers to prolong the barrel maturation through a second winter. This improves the depth, stability and aging potential of the wines. Domaine Matrot is a Domaine that has many holdings of old vine vineyards, therefore the wines show more complexity and concentration. In 2000 Domaine Matrot decided to cultivate all of their wines utilizing organic standards. This wine needs some air to open up so make sure to use a proper Burgundy glass when pouring.

PAZO DE GALEGOS ALBARIÑO 2008. Rias Baixas, Spain

Rias Baixas is the leading DO (Denominacion de Origen: a Spanish controlled appellation) wine zone in northwest Spain, and produces some of the country's best and purest dry, white wines. The vineyards are based on granite infused soil and vines grow under a relatively cool, damp, maritime climate. Albariño is an aromatic, high-quality grape that is produced without any oak treatment. The flavor of Albariño possesses a "green" and juicy acid much like a granny smith apple. The Pazo de Galegos grows further inland which means that this wine has a little more body and power than the Arbariños from the coastal area.

APPLE JAM   MAKES 4 CUPS

Preserving the abundant fruits and vegetables during the season is a great way to enjoy the bounty. Of course, homemade preserves always make nice gifts if you feel like sharing.

3   *pounds tart red apples,*
    such as Jonathan or Empire
¼   *cup fresh lemon juice*
1   *cup water*
3   *cinnamon sticks (optional)*
2   *cups sugar*

Special Equipment:
– *two 1-pint mason jars with lids*
– *candy thermometer*

Wash and chop up the apples, including the skin and seeds. Place the chopped apples in a pot and cover with the lemon juice and 1 cup of water. Cover the pot and simmer over low heat until the apples are tender and cooked through, about 20 minutes. Strain the apples through a cheesecloth or a fine-mesh sieve, pressing gently to extract as much juice as possible but not letting the pulp get through. You should have about 2 cups of juice.

Combine the apple juice, cinnamon sticks (if using) and sugar in a large saucepan and bring the mixture to a boil. Cook the apple mixture until the temperature reaches 220°F on a candy thermometer. Pour the mixture into two clean, sterilized, 1-pint jars and cover with the lids.

If you are making a larger batch and want to keep the jam for a long period of time, place the closed jars of apple jam in a large pot of boiling water to seal the jars. Otherwise, the jam will keep in a refrigerator for about 3 months.

GRAPE MOSTARDA   MAKES 2 CUPS

Mostarda is an Italian condiment made from candied fruit and mustard, traditionally served with rich meats. The grapes are simmered with balsamic vinegar, sugar and spice to create a sweet and spicy garnish great for almost anything.

½   *cup balsamic vinegar*
½   *cup sugar*
1   *tablespoon cracked mustard seeds*
1   *cinnamon stick*
1½ *cups seedless red grapes*
2   *teaspoons dry mustard powder*

Combine the vinegar, sugar, mustard seeds and cinnamon in a saucepan and bring to a boil. Continue boiling until the liquid is reduced by half.

Add the grapes and mustard powder and simmer over low heat for 10 minutes, or until the grapes are just barely cooked through. Transfer the mostarda to clean jars. The mostarda will keep in the refrigerator for 3 months.

CULTURED BUTTER

As a special treat for our guests at Le Bernardin, we began making our own butter a few years ago to serve at the table. To replicate the complex, flavorful cultured butters of Europe, we use both heavy cream and crème fraîche. You may also choose to add a pinch of salt to the butter at the end of the kneading process. It's worth the minimal effort to make this butter at home!

MAKES ABOUT 2 CUPS

1 *quart heavy cream (preferably 40% fat), chilled*
1 *cup crème fraîche*
1 *gallon ice water*

Stir the cold cream and crème fraîche together in the bowl of an electric stand mixer. Using the mixer fitted with the whisk attachment, whip the cream mixture on medium speed for 20 to 25 minutes, or until the fat separates from the liquid, making sure to cover the mixer and bowl with a towel or a piece of plastic wrap.

Drain the butter through a fine-mesh sieve (reserving the buttermilk for later use) and rinse the butter in the ice water. Place the fresh butter on a clean, damp towel and knead on a cold surface to remove the rest of the moisture. Wrap the butter well and refrigerate. For best flavor, allow the butter to warm up to room temperature before serving.

SAUTÉED SHIITAKE MUSHROOMS WITH SAGE

Shiitake mushrooms are some of the easiest and most flavorful mushrooms to find and cook. This earthy herbal side dish only takes about 10 minutes to make.

SERVES 4

2 *tablespoons canola oil*
1½ *pounds shiitake mushroom caps, stems removed*
– *fine sea salt and freshly ground white pepper*
2 *tablespoons chopped fresh sage leaves*
2 *tablespoons unsalted butter*
1 *shallot, finely diced*
1 *garlic clove, finely chopped*

Heat 2 tablespoons of the canola oil in a large sauté pan over high heat. When the oil is almost smoking, add the shiitake mushrooms, season with salt and pepper, and sauté until the mushrooms begin to brown, about 5 minutes. Add the sage, butter, shallots and garlic, then lower the heat and cook until the shallots are tender, about 5 minutes. Serve hot.

SHEEP'S MILK CHEESE SOUFFLÉS

Made with a sharp Manchego cheese from Spain, these individual soufflés are rich and delicious. Make sure to time the soufflés just right so you can serve them straight from the oven and make a great impression.

SERVES 4

3 *tablespoons unsalted butter, plus more for coating soufflé dishes*
¼ *cup fine dried bread crumbs*
3 *tablespoons all purpose flour*
1 *cup whole milk*
2 *large egg yolks*
– *fine sea salt and freshly ground white pepper*
6 *ounces grated Manchego cheese*
4 *large egg whites*

Special Equipment
4 *soufflé dishes, 4-ounce each*

Preheat the oven to 375°F.

Butter four 4-ounce soufflé dishes and sprinkle with the bread crumbs, tilting the dishes to coat completely, tapping out any excess bread crumbs. Arrange the prepared soufflé dishes on a large baking sheet.

Melt 3 tablespoons of the butter in a small saucepan. Whisk in the flour and cook until the flour has absorbed all of the butter, 3 to 5 minutes. Slowly add the milk, whisking constantly until the béchamel sauce thickens enough to coat the back of a spoon. Remove the pan from the heat and let the sauce cool slightly. Place 1 cup of the warm béchamel sauce in a bowl and whisk in the yolks; whisk in the cheese and season with salt and pepper.

Whip the egg whites in a large bowl to soft peaks, fold a fourth of the whites into the cheese mixture, then fold in the remaining whites until the mixture is light and airy. Divide the soufflé batter among the prepared dishes, filling each about three-fourths full. Bake for about 25 minutes, rotating the pan after about 10 minutes, or until they have risen and the tops are golden brown. Serve immediately.

HERB AND SALT-CRUSTED LAMB LOIN   SERVES 4

The dough that encases the lamb loin infuses salt and herbs into the meat in a more subtle way than rubbing the herbs onto the loin itself. The dough also acts as a jacket, protecting the meat as it cooks and keeping it incredibly moist.

3   *cups all purpose flour,*
     plus more for dusting
1½ *cups coarse sea salt*
1½ *tablespoons chopped fresh rosemary*
1   *tablespoon chopped fresh thyme*
3-4 *large egg whites*
2   *tablespoons olive oil*
1   *tablespoon unsalted butter*
–   *fine sea salt and freshly ground*
     black pepper
1   *boneless lamb loin, 1½- to 2-pound,*
     excess fat and silver skin removed
1   *large whole egg, beaten to blend*
½   *cup chicken stock (recipe p. 29)*
1   *rosemary sprig*

Combine 3 cups of the flour with the coarse salt, chopped rosemary and thyme in a large bowl. Gradually add the egg whites, mixing with your hands, until the mixture forms a soft but not sticky dough. Flour your hands, turn the dough out onto a work surface and knead until smooth. Wrap the dough in plastic and let stand at room temperature for at least 2 hours or in the refrigerator for up to 1 day.

Preheat the oven to 450°F. Heat the olive oil and butter in a large sauté pan over high heat. Generously pepper the lamb loin and carefully add the loin to the hot pan. Sear until the loin is golden brown on all sides, about 3 minutes. Remove from the heat and set the lamb loin aside to cool. Reserve the pan.

Flour a large work surface and rolling pin. Place the dough on the floured surface and roll the dough to a 15 x 12-inch rectangle, or large enough to wrap around the lamb loin. Place the seared lamb loin in the center of the dough and wrap the dough around the loin to encase it completely. Brush the edges of the dough with the beaten egg and pinch to seal completely. Place the crusted lamb loin, seam side down, on a baking sheet lined with parchment paper and brush the top with more egg. Bake the lamb for 12 to 15 minutes for medium-rare or until a meat thermometer inserted into the loin registers 115°F. Let the lamb rest at room temperature for at least 10 minutes before cracking open the crust.

While the lamb is resting, heat the reserved pan (used to sear the lamb) over high heat. Deglaze the pan with the chicken stock, add the rosemary sprig, and simmer until the stock is reduced by half, making sure to scrape the bottom and sides of the pan. Season the jus to taste with salt and pepper. Carefully remove the lamb loin from the crust and cut the loin into slices. Arrange the slices of lamb on a platter and serve with the pan jus.

WALNUT BRITTLE MAKES ABOUT 1 ½ POUNDS

Nut brittles are basically a cooked mixture of caramel and nuts that is spread onto a pan
to become hard or "brittle." Walnuts give this brittle a bit of sophistication.

2 *cups sugar*
½ *cup water*
¼ *teaspoon fine sea salt*
¼ *cup unsalted butter*
3 *tablespoons heavy cream*
2 *cups coarsely chopped walnuts*
½ *teaspoon baking soda*

Cover a large baking sheet with foil and lightly butter the foil.

Bring the sugar, water and salt to a boil in a wide saucepan over
medium-high heat, stirring to dissolve the sugar. Brush down the
sides of the pan with water, insert a candy thermometer into the
syrup and boil, without stirring, until the syrup is golden brown
in color and the thermometer registers 340°F.

While the sugar is cooking, melt the butter in a sauté pan over
high heat and cook, whisking constantly, until golden brown and
fragrant, making sure not to burn the butter. Remove the pan
from the heat and whisk in the cream.

Remove the caramel from the heat and quickly stir in the
browned butter mixture, walnuts and baking soda. Quickly
pour the mixture onto the prepared baking sheet. Using a metal
spatula, spread the mixture out to about ¼-inch thickness. Let
the brittle harden, then break it into 2-inch pieces. Serve the
brittle immediately or store it in an airtight container for up to
7 days.

CHOCOLATE SOUFFLÉS SERVES 6

Perhaps the most iconic, decadent dessert is the chocolate soufflé. Soufflés, especially chocolate, make a home dinner party something very special when they are pulled from the oven and served immediately.

1   *cup granulated sugar, plus more for coating soufflé dishes, divided*
½   *cup whole milk*
1   *teaspoon vanilla extract*
½   *cup unsweetened cocoa powder*
2   *teaspoons cornstarch*
–   *unsalted butter for coating soufflé dishes*
¾   *cup egg whites*
–   *confectioners' sugar for dusting*

Special Equipment
6   *soufflé dishes, 8-ounces each*

Combine ½ cup of the granulated sugar with the milk and vanilla in a heavy, nonreactive saucepan and bring to a boil. Meanwhile, sift the cocoa and cornstarch together in a bowl. Gradually whisk the cocoa mixture into the hot milk mixture. Stirring constantly, continue cooking until the chocolate mixture is thickened and returns to a boil. Strain the chocolate mixture through a fine-mesh sieve and into a bowl. Set the bowl over an ice water bath to chill.

While the chocolate base is chilling, preheat the oven to 400°F. Butter four 8-ounce soufflé dishes and sprinkle with granulated sugar, tilting the dishes to coat completely and tapping out any excess. Arrange the prepared soufflé dishes on a large baking sheet.

Place the egg whites in the bowl of an electric mixer fitted with the whisk attachment. Begin whipping the whites, gradually adding the remaining ½ cup of granulated sugar. Continue whipping the whites until soft peaks form. Gently fold one-fourth of the egg whites into the chocolate base to lighten it, then fold in the remaining egg whites. Divide the soufflé batter among the prepared dishes. Tap the dishes to release any large air pockets.

Bake the soufflés for about 8 minutes, or until fully risen. Dust with confectioners' sugar and serve immediately.

Chapter 11

TRADITION

Pocantico Hills, New York

with Chef DAN BARBER of Blue Hill Restaurant.

MUCH OF MY DESIRE TO BECOME A CHEF CAME FROM EARLY EXPERIENCES IN THE KITCHENS OF MY GRANDMOTHER AND MOTHER. Traditional recipes are important maps to follow in order to create something new. Documenting, preparing and sharing not only the recipes but the stories behind those dishes keep them alive; even if a new version of that dish ends up being something quite different, the inspiration is still there.

Chefs are relying more and more on farmers to help dictate how they cook. This is a very interesting shift that is happening all over the country—this reconnecting with the source of the ingredients. In the past, this was always the way to cook, simply because we were bound to what was being grown in our region. Perhaps we sort of forgot this way for a while because it is so easy to get ingredients from all over the world. But there's an important local food movement happening everywhere that pushes us to become reacquainted with where our food comes from and who is producing it. Some chefs are even becoming farmers themselves, not just in California and New England, but all across the United States. Even some New York City chefs are planting little kitchen gardens in tiny courtyards and on rooftops. The connection between products and the plate has always been important, but there seems to be a magnifying glass on it now. It is a return to the traditional way of cooking.

A fine example of this farmer/chef relationship can be witnessed at chef Dan Barber's exquisite restaurant, Blue Hill at Stone Barns. Dan also has a restaurant in New York City called, simply, Blue Hill. A few years ago he partnered with the Stone Barns Agriculture Center, located 30 miles upstate from the city, to open this second restaurant. Most of what is served at both Blue Hill restaurants comes from the greenhouses and pastures at Stone Barns, and Dan has become more and more involved with the actual operation of the farm. He took me on a tour of the facility in the late fall, and while I thought the farm might not be in a big production mode because of the season, I soon realized that there is something vital and exciting going on there all the time.

The greenhouses are huge and the farmers are constantly working with new varieties, heirloom seeds and soil management. They compare the previous season's

notes and experience with what they are doing presently in order to come up with the most delicious, healthy vegetables that they can. They are finding that everything factors into taste, and the lines between chef and farmer become blurred because Dan believes that the farmer is just as responsible for how the resulting dish tastes as is the chef.

Outside the greenhouses, there are about 60 acres of pasture and forests where cows, sheep, pigs and chickens are raised. Using the traditional technique of rotating livestock from pasture to pasture and sometimes into the woods is a holistic and natural approach to animal husbandry. For example, groups of sheep are put out into lush pastures where they are allowed to eat the tops of the fresh new grass, which is also the tastiest. But before they can eat the grass down to the roots, chickens are brought in and the sheep are moved to another pasture. This rotation simulates a very natural occurrence—in nature, birds follow big animals around since the larger animals eat the tall grass, making it easier for the birds to find insects, their choice source of food. In turn, the chickens help spread the manure around, which will help fertilize the field. Pigs are foragers and rooters, and they use their strong snouts to root around in and stir up the ground—almost like a tiller. The pigs are gathered into certain areas of grass for a while and then moved to the wooded areas of the farm to fatten up on the different vegetation there, including acorns. All of these processes are good for the farm environment and dramatically impact the taste of the animal. Their flavors are complex and natural—very different from animals raised in confinement feedlots.

Dan is an accomplished, James Beard award-winning chef, and his kitchen, while located in a historic place, is modern and state-of-the-art. Dan also likes to utilize some very modern equipment and techniques alongside his traditional sensibilities. He showed me how he uses an immersion circulator to cook the perfect poached egg inside the shell. The circulator keeps moving water at a constant

STONE BARNS CENTER FOR FOOD AND AGRICULTURE

The mission of this unique, nonprofit, member-driven collaboration is to celebrate, teach, and advance community-based food production and enjoyment, from farm to classroom to table. The center is considered a campus that includes a farm, a kitchen and classrooms. Offering workshops and discussions that cover a range of topics from animal husbandry to children's cooking classes, Stone Barns is a valuable resource and an example of sustainability in a beautiful, historic setting. Chef Dan Barber's incredible restaurant, Blue Hill at Stone Barns, is located on the campus. Dinner there, after a day of learning about food and farming, is the perfect way to truly enjoy farm-to-table eating in its most honest form.
www.stonebarnscenter.org
www.bluehillfarm.com

FARM TO TABLE AT HOME

The act of growing your own food and eventually cooking and eating it is the best way to connect with the earth and the food itself; it takes the experience beyond just feeding yourself. While some people have room for a backyard garden, some only have room for a small planter on a window-sill. Even if all you have is one pot of herbs, just using a pinch from a plant that you have taken care of changes the way you feel about the food you cook—it adds a layer of pride and connection with nature.

–Choose herbs that you use often. Some great ones to plant in a container are mint, sage, rosemary, thyme and parsley.
–Select a container that is at least 4" deep. If you are planting a mixture, make sure to get one that is big enough for the plants to expand into as they grow.
–Herbs like lots of light; place the plants in a sunny window or use a grow light.
–Drainage is very important for the plants to stay healthy, so select some pots that have good drainage holes in the bottom. You can also put a one-inch layer of pebbles in the bottom of the pot to help drain the excess water.
–Cutting the herbs a little at a time, as you cook, will prune the plants so that they will stay small enough for your kitchen. Be careful not to cut too much off at one time or they will not grow back.

temperature. When food is cooked "sous vide" (under pressure), vacuum-sealed items are cooked in a water bath and the circulator aids in maintaining a constant temperature. With the eggs, Dan simply leaves them in their shells, puts them in a 62°C water bath for 20 minutes, and the result is the perfect texture for a soft-boiled egg. This technique, along with the freshness of the pastured chicken egg, produced one of the most delicious eggs I have ever eaten, and very much reminded me of the eggs my family enjoyed while I was growing up in France.

An important tradition at Le Bernardin, as well as at many other restaurants, is the "family meal." This is the time, in between kitchen prep and dinner service, when the staff shares a meal together. Each day, our sauté cook prepares a simple and hearty meal that will sustain the staff through the busy service time. Many times, the recipes that are cooked for this meal are what would be considered "comfort food." I suppose many of the recipes are dishes that cooks have learned from their parents and have been cooking all their lives: pasta or posole or some other regional dish inspired by where they're from. This point in the workday is also an opportunity to take a few minutes to socialize with each other or cover important information for that day's service.

Recently, I was inspired to make something that I have not had for a very long time—stuffed capon. Capons are typically bigger than chickens and have a slightly different flavor. My family would eat capon for a holiday meal or for a very special Sunday dinner. My grandmother is an inspiration to me because of the way she put recipes together. She had her own unique ways of preparing food. She was very focused and, while her technique might not be the way a trained chef would cook, it always worked and actually gave the food a special quality— her dishes have lots of soul. I wanted to share this inspiration and tradition with the staff by making capon for the family meal. Since capon was for special occasions, I wanted to use foie gras and truffles in the stuffing—wonderful ingredients to celebrate a meal.

While traveling has inspired new ideas and introduced me to new technology, food tradition is very important to who I am—the foods I grew up with and the things I enjoyed as a child. These experiences shape the way I look at cuisine, inspire our menu at Le Bernardin, and influence what I cook at home with my young son.

FAMILY MEAL at Le BERNARDIN.

ROASTED CHICKEN WITH ZA'ATAR STUFFING   SERVES 4

A good roast chicken is one of my favorite things to cook and eat. Every cook should know how to roast a chicken properly. The stuffing in this recipe contains a fantastic Middle Eastern spice blend called za'atar, which is a combination of sesame seeds and dried herbs such as basil, thyme and oregano.

1   *4-pound chicken*
1½ *cups diced crusty bread*
2   *tablespoons chopped fresh Italian parsley*
1   *tablespoon minced garlic plus 1 head of garlic, cloves separated*
2   *teaspoons za'atar*
1   *teaspoon lemon zest*
¼   *cup plus 2 tablespoons olive oil*
–   *fine sea salt and freshly ground black pepper*

Special Equipment
–   *kitchen string*

Preheat the oven to 450°F. Rinse the chicken and pat dry. Remove the wings and reserve.

Combine the bread, parsley, minced garlic, za'atar and lemon zest in a mixing bowl and toss with ¼ cup of the olive oil to coat evenly. Season the stuffing with salt and pepper.

Season the cavity of the chicken with salt and pepper and fill with the stuffing. Tie the legs together with kitchen string. Season the bird on the outside with salt and pepper and drizzle with the remaining 2 tablespoons of olive oil.

Place the wings in a roasting pan and place the chicken on top of the wings. Roast for 20 minutes. Reduce the oven temperature to 350°F and add the garlic cloves to the roasting pan. Continue roasting for 25 to 30 minutes, or until the juices run clear when the leg is pierced. Transfer the chicken to a platter and let it rest for at least 10 minutes.

Carve the chicken by removing the leg and thigh at the joint, then run the carving knife down one side of the breast bone and continue by following the rib cage, lifting the breast meat away from the bone. Repeat on the other side of the breast bone, removing the second breast. Slice the breast meat and leg meat.

Place 2 slices each of breast and leg meat on each plate and spoon some of the stuffing alongside. Spoon some of the pan drippings over the chicken and serve immediately.

WINE PAIRINGS

Many recipes are inspired by memory and tradition. It is important to incorporate traditional recipes and techniques into cooking but it is also fun to experiment a little. This roast chicken recipe includes an exotic spice called za'atar, which ended up making the dish very robust and exciting.
The two wines featured have roots in very traditional winemaking regions, and their producers understand the importance of old world style without alienating the flavors that go so well with worldly cuisine.

LUCIANO SANDRONE DOLCETTO D'ALBA 2007. Piedmont, Italy

The Piedmont region of Italy is quite a fantastic area with its breathtaking views of the majestic snow-covered Swiss and Italian Alps and, of course, the famously aromatic white truffles that grow there. Dolcetto, a varietal common in the Piedmont, is wine for everyday drinking. It is often soft, round, fruit-driven and fragrant, with flavors of licorice and almonds. Sandrone is often seen as a modernist in the Piedmont because he opts for shorter macerations and uses some new oak in his wines. His wines are often rich but very polished.

JOSEPH DROUHIN GEVREY-CHAMBERTIN 2005/6. Burgundy, France

Gevrey-Chambertin is a small town in the Côte de Nuits producing some of Burgundy's most famous red wines made from Pinot Noir grapes. In 1847, Gevrey annexed the name of its finest vineyard, Chambertin. These Pinot Noirs are generally deeper in color and are a little firmer than the wines of their rivals from neighboring villages. Here in the 'Homeland' of Pinot Noir it is all about the terroir. Of course there are many great, top-level wines from all over the world, but once you have the luck to drink great red Burgundy at its peak, you will never forget that experience! Joseph Drouhin is a négociant in Burgundy who produces wonderful wines for a great value.

PERFECT MANHATTAN   MAKES 1 COCKTAIL

A cocktail dating from the mid-1800s, the Manhattan is always a good choice—
well balanced and classic.

2 *ounces bourbon*
½ *ounce dry vermouth*
½ *ounce sweet vermouth*
– *3 to 4 dashes Peychaud's bitters*
– *ice cubes*
– *morello cherry packed in light syrup*
   for garnish

Combine the bourbon, both vermouths, and bitters in a mixing glass with ice. Stir well and strain the cocktail into a martini glass or rocks glass. Garnish with the cherry and serve.

DEVILED EGGS WITH SMOKED SALMON   SERVES 4

Deviled eggs are a fun way to offer an appetizer that guests can just pick up and eat in a couple of bites. Hard-cooked eggs go well with so many different flavors. Smoked salmon and mayonnaise make these deviled eggs a little richer.

6 *large eggs*
2 *ounces smoked salmon, diced*
2 *tablespoons crème fraîche*
1 *tablespoon sliced chives*
2 *teaspoons Dijon mustard*
– *fine sea salt and freshly ground*
   black pepper
– *cayenne pepper*
1 *lemon, cut in half*
– *paprika, for garnish*

Place the eggs in a large saucepan and cover with water. Bring the water to a boil, then cover and remove from the heat. Let the eggs sit in the hot water, covered, for 12 to 15 minutes. Drain the hot water and run cold water over the boiled eggs until cool.

Peel the eggs and cut each egg in half lengthwise. Gently remove the yolks from the center and place them in a small mixing bowl. Set the egg white halves aside.

Add the smoked salmon, crème fraîche, chives and mustard to the egg yolks and stir to combine. Season to taste with salt, black pepper and cayenne pepper. Squeeze enough of the lemon juice into the yolk mixture to season to taste.

Spoon the yolk mixture back into the egg whites. Garnish with paprika and serve.

CLASSIC BEEF TARTARE

The finest grade of beef is best eaten barely cooked or raw—the flavor really shines through. This iconic recipe mixes beef tenderloin, mustard, red onion and cornichons, all chopped together and topped with quail egg yolks. Serve it with crusty rustic bread.

SERVES 4

- 1 *pound beef tenderloin, sinew removed, meat finely chopped*
- 2 *tablespoons canola oil*
- 2 *tablespoons chopped cornichons*
- 2 *tablespoons chopped fresh Italian parsley*
- 2 *tablespoons fresh lemon juice*
- 1 *tablespoon chopped capers*
- 1 *tablespoon Dijon mustard*
- 1 *tablespoon minced red onion*
- 2 *teaspoons Worcestershire sauce*
- 1 *teaspoon Tabasco sauce, or to taste*
- – *fine sea salt and freshly ground black pepper*
- 4 *quail egg yolks*
- 12 *pieces toasted country bread, warm*

Combine the beef, canola oil, cornichons, parsley, lemon juice, capers, Dijon mustard, onion, Worcestershire sauce and Tabasco in a mixing bowl. Season to taste with salt, pepper and more Tabasco, if desired, and gently toss with a fork to combine.

Place a 3-inch ring mold in the center of a plate and gently pack about 4 tablespoons of tartare into the ring mold, then lift off the ring mold. Make a small indentation in the middle of the tartare on the plate and place 1 egg yolk in the indentation. Repeat on 3 more plates with the remaining tartare and egg yolks. Serve immediately with the warm toast.

ROMAINE SALAD WITH GARLIC VINAIGRETTE

I love this simple salad; it always reminds me of my grandparents. During the day, my grandfather would collect the vegetables from the garden for our meal. Back at the house, my grandmother would prepare this delicious salad dressing.

SERVES 4

- 1 *tablespoon sherry vinegar*
- 1 *garlic clove, minced (about 1 teaspoon)*
- ¼ *teaspoon Dijon mustard*
- – *fine sea salt and freshly ground black pepper*
- 3 *tablespoons olive oil*
- 2 *heads romaine hearts, trimmed and torn into bite-size pieces*
- ½ *small onion, very thinly sliced*

Using a fork, mix the vinegar, garlic and mustard in a bowl to blend. Let stand for at least 10 minutes to marinate.

Season the vinaigrette with salt and pepper and slowly drizzle in the olive oil while mixing to blend.

Toss the romaine lettuce and sliced onion in a large bowl with the vinaigrette and serve immediately.

COQ AU VIN

Traditionally, a tougher bird—or one that wasn't so fat—was braised with *mirepoix* (celery, carrots and onions), lardoons or bacon, and red wine. The long slow simmer would tenderize the meat. A beautiful, plump chicken makes this classic pairing even more delicious.

SERVES 4

- 1 *whole chicken, approx. 3 to 4 pounds, cut into 8 pieces*
- – *fine sea salt and freshly ground black pepper*
- 1 *tablespoon all-purpose flour plus more for dusting*
- ¼ *cup canola oil*
- 1 *slice smoked bacon (optional)*
- ½ *cup diced celery*
- ½ *cup diced onion*
- ½ *cup diced peeled carrot*
- 3 *ounces button mushrooms, washed and diced*
- 2 *garlic cloves, sliced*
- ½ *cup brandy*
- 1 *750-ml bottle dry red wine*
- 1 *tablespoon tomato paste*
- 2 *thyme sprigs*
- 1 *cup reduced chicken stock (recipe p. 29)*
- – *egg noodles*

Lay the chicken pieces on a cutting board or baking sheet, then season the chicken with salt and pepper and lightly dust with flour. Heat the canola oil in a heavy stock pot over medium heat. In batches, add the chicken pieces and cook until the skin is golden brown and crispy. Turn the chicken pieces over and continue cooking until golden brown. Remove the chicken from the pot and discard all but 1 tablespoon of oil. Cook the bacon in the pot (if using it) until it is crisp. Add the celery, onion, carrot, mushrooms and garlic, and cook until the vegetables are lightly caramelized, 5 to 7 minutes.

Deglaze the pan with the brandy and return the browned chicken to the pot. Stir in 1 tablespoon of flour, then the red wine, tomato paste, thyme and chicken stock. Bring the liquid to a boil, then reduce the heat to low and simmer for about 2 hours, or until the chicken is very tender and starts falling off the bone.

Carefully transfer the chicken pieces to a bowl and cover to keep warm. Simmer the braising liquid until it is reduced by half and thickened slightly, about 10 minutes. Return the chicken to the sauce and season to taste with salt and pepper.

Meanwhile, cook the noodles in a large pot of boiling salted water until tender but still firm to the bite. Drain the noodles and divide them among 4 plates. Top with the chicken and sauce and serve.

RATATOUILLE

A favorite French recipe, this dish includes a variety of summer vegetables, such as bell peppers, onion, tomatoes, zucchini and eggplant with herbs that are typically grown in Provence.

SERVES 4

¼ cup extra virgin olive oil
1 large onion, cut into ½-inch dice
1 red bell pepper, cut into ½-inch dice
1 banana pepper, seeded and cut
  into ½-inch dice
4 garlic cloves, thinly sliced
1 tablespoon tomato paste
3 tomatoes, seeded and cut into
  ½-inch dice
2 small zucchini, cut into ½-inch dice
1 medium eggplant, peeled and cut
  into ½-inch dice
1 teaspoon dried oregano
¼ cup grated Parmesan cheese
¼ cup julienned fresh basil

Heat the olive oil in a Dutch oven over medium-high heat. Add the onion, red pepper, banana pepper and garlic and sauté until tender, 5 to 7 minutes.

Add the tomato paste and continue cooking for 3 to 5 minutes.

Add the tomatoes, zucchini, eggplant and oregano and cook until tender, about 10 minutes, adding water as necessary.

Season to taste with salt and pepper and serve hot with Parmesan and basil on top.

BOULANGERE POTATOES WITH BAY LEAF

Arranging sliced potatoes in overlapping layers with onions, garlic, herbs and butter is a very traditional way to prepare potatoes. Baking them together slowly makes a tender casserole.

SERVES 4

3 tablespoons unsalted butter
1½ pounds russet potatoes,
  peeled and thinly sliced
1 onion, thinly sliced
2 garlic cloves, sliced
1 teaspoon ground bay leaf
– fine sea salt and freshly ground
  white pepper .
½ cup chicken stock (recipe p. 29)

Preheat the oven to 350°F.

Coat a 9x9-inch casserole dish with some of the butter, then form one layer of potato and onion slices in the dish in an overlapping pattern. Top with a few slices of garlic and sprinkle with some of the ground bay leaf. Season with salt and pepper and continue layering the potatoes, onion, garlic, and ground bay leaf, seasoning each layer with salt and pepper and ending with a layer of potatoes on top. Dot the top with the remaining butter and cover with the chicken stock. Bake the casserole in the oven for 1½ to 2 hours, uncovered, or until a paring knife is easily inserted into the potatoes.

ROASTED CAPON WITH MUSHROOM-TRUFFLE STUFFING

A capon is a large bird with tender meat. My grandmother used to make a stuffed capon for special family meals, such as holidays or birthdays. This recipe pays homage to my grandmother and integrates some luxurious ingredients, such as truffles and foie gras.

MAKES 6 SERVINGS

1   *6-pound capon*
1   *cup ½-inch cubes fresh white bread*
⅓   *cup whole milk*
6   *ounces chopped chicken liver*
½   *pound mixed fresh mushrooms,*
    such as chanterelles, porcini and
    cremini, cleaned and diced
1   *ounce black truffles, diced*
1   *large egg, lightly beaten*
2   *tablespoons chopped fresh*
    Italian parsley
2   *tablespoons diced shallot*
1½ *tablespoons minced garlic*
1   *tablespoon duck fat or*
    unsalted butter, melted
½   *teaspoon fresh thyme leaves*
–   *fine sea salt and freshly ground*
    white pepper
2   *cups chicken stock (recipe p. 29)*

Special Equipment
–   *kitchen string*
–   *trussing needle*

Preheat the oven to 400°F. Rinse the capon and pat dry. Remove the wings and reserve.

Soak the bread in the milk in a bowl until the milk is absorbed. Squeeze out the excess milk from the bread and place the bread in a large bowl. Mix in the chicken liver, mushrooms, truffles, egg, parsley, shallot, garlic, duck fat, thyme and season to taste with salt and pepper. Season the cavity of the capon with salt and pepper and fill with the stuffing.

Thread a trussing needle with a piece of kitchen string that is at least 18 inches long. Sew the opening of the capon closed by starting at one side of the top of the cavity opening and crossing the string down through the opposite side, pulling the string tight and repeating on the other side of the opening to crisscross the string. Finally, thread the string through the top of the opening and pass the needle through the bottom of the opening, pulling tight and closing the cavity completely. Tie the legs together. Season the capon on the outside with salt and pepper.

Put the reserved wings in a roasting pan and place the capon on top of the wings. Roast for 90 minutes, or until the juices run clear when the leg is pierced and the stuffing reaches 150°F. Transfer the capon to a platter and let it rest for at least 10 minutes.

Place the roasting pan over high heat and add the chicken stock to deglaze the pan and stir the browned bits from the bottom of the pan. Bring the stock to a boil, then remove the pan from the heat. Strain the pan juices into a small saucepan. Season to taste with salt and pepper.

Carve the capon by removing the leg and thigh at the joint, then run the carving knife down one side of the breast bone. Continue by following the rib cage, lifting the breast meat away from the bone. Repeat on the other side of the breast bone, removing the second breast. Slice the breast meat and leg meat.

Place 2 slices each of breast and leg meat on each plate and spoon some of the stuffing alongside. Spoon some of the pan sauce over and pass the extra pan sauce at the table. Serve immediately.

255

APPLE GALETTE

The method used for cooking the apples in this recipe is a simple way to generate a deep flavor and richness simply by adding sugar, cinnamon, vanilla and a slow cooking time. Sandwiched between two sheets of puff pastry, the layer of apples becomes enclosed as the pastry cooks around it.

SERVES 6-8

½ cup granulated sugar
– water, as needed
3 tablespoons unsalted butter, approx.
½ teaspoon ground cinnamon
½ vanilla bean, split lengthwise
5 Granny Smith apples, peeled and cored
1 sheet frozen puff pastry dough, cut into a 9-inch circle, kept in the freezer
1 egg, slightly beaten

Place a silicon baking mat (such as a Silpat) or a large sheet of parchment paper on a flat work surface, and have ready another mat or sheet of parchment paper. Place the sugar in a heavy saucepan and add enough water to cover the sugar. Cook the sugar, without stirring, until it turns into a dark caramel, about 10 minutes. Remove the pan from the heat and stir in 2 tablespoons of the butter and cinnamon. Scrape the seeds from the vanilla bean into the caramel and stir to blend. Pour the caramel mixture onto the center of the mat or parchment paper on the work surface, then place the second mat or sheet of parchment paper on top. Using a rolling pin, flatten the caramel carefully and allow it to cool and set. Break the caramel mixture into small pieces, then place them in a food processor and grind them into a fine powder.

Preheat the oven to 325°F. Lightly coat an 8-inch round cake pan with the remaining 1 tablespoon of butter and sprinkle in a little of the cinnamon-caramel powder. Slice the apples crosswise, as thinly as possible. Arrange half of the apple slices over the cinnamon-caramel powder in the pan, forming one layer and overlapping slightly. Cover the apples with a few spoonfuls of the cinnamon-caramel powder and repeat with the remaining apple slices and caramel powder.

Cover the pan with aluminum foil and bake for 1 hour, or until the apples are cooked through, tender, and just slightly caramelized. Remove the foil and bake an additional 20 minutes, allowing the excess moisture to evaporate. Transfer the pan to a rack and allow the apples to cool. Meanwhile, increase the oven temperature to 400°F.

Place the cold puff pastry round, centered, on top of the pan over the cooled apples. Cover with a large sheet of parchment paper and top with a baking sheet, then invert the apple cake onto the parchment-lined baking sheet. If necessary, recenter the inverted cake pan on top of the puff pastry dough, leaving a 1-inch border of dough around the pan. Remove the cake pan, revealing the layers of baked apples. Lightly brush the exposed dough with the beaten egg and bake for 20 to 25 minutes, or until the dough is golden brown and has puffed evenly around the apple filling. Cool slightly, then slice into wedges and serve.

AN EVOLVED KITCHEN: THE NEW LIVING ROOM

Since I have decided to start designing kitchens with Poggenpohl, I thought it might be useful to share my philosophy on home kitchens that may help you whether you're installing a brand new one, renovating your current kitchen or even just reorganizing.

The home kitchen is not just a place where meals are cooked and dishes are washed, but it should be the thriving heart of any home, where a family bonds, guests are entertained and people live. For me and my family, it is the social center of the home. I believe the kitchen should not only look great and feel exquisite, but become a true expression of any cook's expertise, style and taste.

The kitchen is more than just a tool. Kitchens are not for display; they are for living in, for hosting dinner parties, for experimenting, for making mistakes in. And most importantly... for cooking!

MISE EN PLACE

Literally translated as "putting in place," *mise en place* is a term used in restaurant kitchens to describe the layout and preparation used by line cooks at their stations. It is this experience and insight that I bring into how a home kitchen functions best and it has everything to do with efficiency and organization. There is only one way to get to the soulful and creative headspace that a chef requires, and that is through a flawlessly performing kitchen. Flexibility and sensibility of layout is a must whether you're in a large home or a small apartment, the *mise en place* system has the solution that will make every meal an effortless pleasure to prepare. And a happy cook is a good cook!

Chapter 12

CAYMAN COOKOUT

Cayman Islands

CAYMAN COOKOUT
HOSTED BY ERIC RIPERT

Gala Dinner
Sunday, January 17th, 2010 – The Ritz-Carlton, Grand Cayman

Kumamoto Oyster, Lemon Caper Foam,
Iberico Chip Tuna Cracker with Ginger Sabayon
Created by Chef Richard Brower & Chef Luis Lugan

Sweet Corn Vichyssoise with Bacon / Jalapeño Wrapped Texas Quail,
Smoked Tomatoes, Grilled Salsify & Cilantro Cream
Created by Chef Dean Fearing

Razor Clams with Chorizo Sauce
Created by Chef Anthony Bourdain

Seared Langoustine, Baby Spinach and Mache, Shaved Foie Gras,
White Balsamic Vinaigrette
Created by Chef Eric Ripert

Local Conch, Pork Belly & Napa Cabbage with Kim Chi Juice
Created by Chef David Chang

Wild Turbot: Shellfish, Parsnip, Chamomile
Created by Chef Grant Achatz

Mar y Montaña
Created by Chef José Andrés

Warm Pineapple Meringue with Malted Cilantro Ice Cream
Created by Chef Alex Grunert

Petit Fours: Chocolate Hazelnut Crunch, Fresh Mint Macaroon,
Coconut Paté des Fruits
Created by Chef Giuliana Tomatis

PROFESSIONAL CHEFS VERY RARELY GET A CHANCE TO COOK TOGETHER OR EVEN JUST HANG OUT. WE KNOW OF EACH OTHER, READ ABOUT EACH OTHER, AND MAY CROSS PATHS AT SPECIAL ONE-DAY EVENTS, BUT USUALLY WE ARE AT AN EVENT TO WORK AND DON'T HAVE ANY TIME TO REALLY VISIT. A couple of years after I opened Blue, my restaurant at The Ritz-Carlton on Grand Cayman Island, Michael Ryan, the owner of the Ritz, and I started brainstorming about what we could do on the island to get some chefs together to have fun and interact. It made sense to us to stage a food and wine event just after the winter holidays. It's nice to go some-where warm during winter, and since our own restaurants are not quite as busy after the holiday season, January seemed like the perfect time.

The idea was to stage an event where we would invite chefs to lead a couple of cooking demonstrations or a discussion about food, and then, at the end of the event, there would be a big gala dinner where all of the chefs would cook together. The event, now known as the Cayman Cookout, has taken place for a few years and has proven to be a success. Not only does it bring people to the island for the event, but it offers chefs the opportunity to relax for a few days and exchange ideas and get to know each other better.

January of 2010 was an extremely cold winter for most of the United States, but the temperature on Grand Cayman was perfect—warm and sunny. Each year, we try to bring together some of the best and most intriguing chefs and wine profes-sionals to be a part of the event. The collaboration of so many talented food and wine professionals adds up to an interesting and inspirational program for the attending public, all amidst a surreal setting. Demonstration tents are set up right on the beach, so it's a lot of fun to sit down for a demo or wine tasting, be in the sand and see the clear, blue Caribbean sea water just a few feet away. The event, because it is relatively small, is also a great chance for the public to meet and mingle with some great chefs.

Guests and chefs alike enjoy taking advantage of some of the island sports, like snorkeling and scuba diving, paddle boarding and kayaking. One of the most exciting things to do on the islands is take a boat to a place called Stingray City. It is a very special and specific place just off the beach where stingrays gather

261

and swim in large packs with people. Many years ago, commercial fishermen would utilize a natural break in the barrier reef that circles the island to get to the open sea. After a long day of fishing, the boats would come back through the reef opening to get to shore. Along the way, the fishermen were working to get the fish cleaned and ready for market, and they would dump the fish parts out into the shallow water. The stingrays liked to eat what the fishermen were throwing over and they got used to being fed each day. Generations of stingrays have learned that this is a place where they would be fed, so they gather in swarms in this one spot. Essentially, these rays are tame because they are fed by people and they are around people so often. Typically, it is not a good idea to swim with rays but these are gentle and will even let you catch and hold them. They are magnificent creatures,and it is an awesome feeling to be in that beautiful water with such powerful and graceful animals.

This particular year at the cookout, I invited a group of chefs who really inspire me. One of my good friends is Anthony Bourdain who, for many years, was the chef at the much-loved New York brasserie, Les Halles. For the past few years, Anthony has been busy writing and traveling the world, gathering material for his hit television show, *No Reservations*. Tony has invited me to tag along with him on some of his adventures, and I was very happy to have him come to the Cayman Cookout this year. People flock to him and want to gather around him to see what he will say and hear the stories that he tells. He is a talented and funny guy and, after all the recent fame and attention he has received, he is still the same genuine guy that I have always known.

José Andrés is a fantastic chef who is originally from just outside of Barcelona, Spain. It was there, at the young age of 15, where José began cooking. He developed his skills cooking classic Spanish cuisine but began to view the potential of cuisine differently when he started working with famed Spanish chef Ferran Adrià at El Bulli. Making his way to the U.S. and to Washington, D.C., José led the kitchen at Jaleo, creating one of the first critically acclaimed tapas restaurants in the country. Now José owns several restaurants in D.C. including Café Atlántico and Minibar—a six-seat showcase for his fantastical, ultra-modern cuisine—along with Bazaar in Los Angeles. It is impressive how José is able to blur the lines between very classic, old-world flavor and cutting-edge techniques of cooking and plating. He is one of the liveliest, most upbeat chefs I have ever known.

GRILLING with ANTHONY BOURDAIN.

ON the BEACH with JOSÉ ANDRÉS.

SWIMMING with STINGRAYS.

Chef Dean Fearing lives and works in Dallas, Texas. His restaurant, Fearing's, is heralded as a great example of innovative Southwestern cuisine. Dean grew up in Virginia with grandmothers who loved to cook. He spent a lot of time learning from them and still considers their instructions and recipes to be some of the most influential inspirations of his culinary life. With this in common, we have fun exchanging stories about watching our grandmothers cook and how their spirits still influence the way we cook. He is a true Southern gentleman and a great chef.

Grant Achatz and his Chicago restaurant, Alinea, have made a definite mark on American cuisine. Chef Achatz is intrigued with the science of food and technique and presents his progressive cuisine in a sophisticated way. Although he is still young, Grant has received many accolades and worldwide recognition as one of the most cutting-edge chefs of the world. But he has also dealt with some serious struggles. A few years ago, he was diagnosed with a type of mouth cancer that could have permanently damaged his sense of taste. He explained to me that he is now cancer-free and has fully recovered his sense of taste. It was incredibly inspiring to hear about his struggle and how he learned from it. I am very happy for his good health and continued professional success.

David Chang is one of the most talked-about chefs in the United States right now. His wildly successful East Village restaurant, Momofuku, has grown into a family of five New York City restaurants, ranging from the original noodle bar to a fourteen-seat fine dining restaurant. I have been around David in social settings and he is always ready to have a good time and enjoy himself. When we sat down for a chat in the Caymans, it was surprising to me to find out that he is very intense in the kitchen. He strives for perfection and wants his staff to continue to come up with the best food that they can create each day. Of course, this is the hope of every chef, and David is certainly producing some of the most delicious and interesting food in Manhattan.

We all had fun getting to know each other, relaxing and spending time with our families at the beach, but we also had some cooking to do. The resort is a very beautiful piece of property, located on the stretch of waterfront known as Seven Mile Beach. Also on that beach are some really fun, casual beach bars. On one night of the event, Anthony Bourdain and I staged a "steak frites cookoff" using

CHEF DAVID CHANG.

CHEF GRANT ACHATZ.

CHEF DEAN FEARING.

some huge grills positioned right on the beach at Calico Jack's. Tony and I, in the past, have had a lot of fun challenging each other in this way. We decided to cook back to back and let the people decide. While we were cooking, people were eating tastes of our steaks while drinking and comparing notes. Anthony and I were kidding around with each other, making fun and criticizing each other's cooking. During the cookout, all the other chefs ended up joining us at the grills—it was a blast.

The final night of the event was our gala dinner, held in the dining room of Blue. The kitchen at Blue is big and very well appointed. The staff knows how to make everything run very smoothly. For the dinner, each of the guest chefs was responsible for one of the courses. Our afternoon of prep time was a bit intense, but it was fun for us to be in the same kitchen cooking together. It was crowded with all of the line cooks, sous chefs, prep cooks and the rest of the staff, but all this activity fills a kitchen with energy. Honestly, a big dinner like that is like staging a Broadway show; everything must go out on time and be perfect.

A camaraderie develops between cooks during an event like the Cayman Cookout and it is a lot of fun. Everyone helped each other and there were no egos. José Andrés, even though he had a very intense course to prepare, brought out an entire Iberico ham to slice as a "snack" for the chefs. Along with that, he opened Champagne and caviar. The spirit was celebratory, and indulging in José's decadent gifts was a nice way to come together with food and drink before we had to really start cooking. Being in the kitchen like that, with so many respected chefs, was humbling in a way. When I looked down the line at all of those amazing cooks working together, I was struck with how much of an honor it was to be there with them, cooking a beautiful and special meal in such a wonderful place.

MY GOOD FRIEND, ANTHONY BOURDAIN.

AT the BEACH COOKOUT with
GEORGE McNeil and DAVID CHANG.

JOSÉ'S IBERICO HAM.

JOSÉ GRILLING SPANISH PORK.

GRAND CAYMAN.

with GRANT ACHATZ.

recipes

CAYMAN COOKOUT

—————————————————

SHRIMP IN COCONUT CURRY SAUCE

Perhaps it is the position of the islands along the spice route in the Caribbean Sea that gave Caymanians access to exotic spices, or maybe it's due to the British influence on the island, but either way, it is quite common to find Indian-inspired dishes on the island. This shrimp curry is influenced by some very delicious seafood curries that I have enjoyed on the islands.

SERVES 4

2	*tablespoons canola oil*
1	*shallot, thinly sliced*
2	*garlic cloves, thinly sliced*
1	*stalk lemongrass, thinly sliced*
2	*tablespoons thinly sliced fresh ginger*
2	*teaspoons Thai red curry paste*
1	*teaspoon Madras curry powder*
½	*cup chicken stock (recipe p.29)*
1	*cup unsweetened coconut milk*
–	*fine sea salt and freshly ground black pepper*
1½	*pounds large shrimp, peeled and deveined*
¼	*cup fresh lime juice*
½	*cup fresh basil, julienned*

Heat the canola oil in a saucepan over medium heat. Add the shallot, garlic, lemongrass and ginger and sauté until softened. Add the Thai curry paste and curry powder and stir to combine. Add the chicken stock and simmer for about 10 minutes, until lightly reduced. Add the coconut milk and simmer for 5 more minutes for the flavors to come together. Remove the curry sauce from the heat and season to taste with salt and pepper. Strain the sauce through a fine-mesh sieve into another saucepan.

Season the shrimp with salt and pepper and add the shrimp to the curry sauce. Bring the curry sauce to a simmer and cook just until the shrimp start to turn opaque, about 5 minutes. Stir in the lime juice to taste. Divide the curry among 4 bowls, then garnish with the basil and serve immediately.

Note: This curry sauce can be served with a simple piece of sautéed fish or chicken.

WINE PAIRINGS

The inspiration for the Shrimp Curry recipe came from some time spent in the Cayman Islands where we prepared the curry to go with local snapper. There is certainly some Indian influence in the cuisine of the Caribbean (most likely because of their position in the original spice route) and curry ends up being used often as well as ginger, coconut, basil and hot peppers. These flavors are typical of tropical food and both the Riesling and the Viognier, with their refreshing qualities and a little bit of residual sugar, really compliment the dish.

EROICA RIESLING. Columbia Valley, Washington

The Riesling grape variety is without a doubt one of the greatest, yet at the same time, most under-appreciated varieties. Riesling always triggers a sweetness that is, most of the time, the decided style of a wine maker or perhaps their expression. Rieslings can be totally dry but keep in mind that completely dry wines are very often hard to match with food, therefore a tiny amount of residual sugar brings a lot of harmony into a pairing. Eroica is joint venture between the famous German Riesling producer Ernst Loosen and Chateau St. Michelle from the Columbia Valley in Washington state. Eroica is certainly one of the best U.S. Rieslings.

STARLITE VINEYARDS VIOGNIER
Alexander Valley, Sonoma, California

The origin of Viognier is unknown and is assumed to be an ancient varietal. The most famous appelation for this varietal are the very steep sites of the Rhone Valley's Condrieu and Chateau Grillet. Starlite Vineyards has produced quite a pure and impressive Viognier that is full bodied with a fresh acid and typical spices, which are very distinct. The Starlite winery is a family owned winery located in the Alexander Valley in Sonoma County.

273

CARIBBEAN FRIED RICE

A perfect side dish for fish or chicken, this flavorful rice includes herbs and tropical fruit
such as mango and banana. It also has a bit of cayenne pepper to add some heat.

SERVES 4 TO 6

1½ *cups uncooked basmati rice*
 – *fine sea salt and freshly ground
   black pepper*
4 *tablespoons olive oil*
3 *tablespoons sliced scallions*
1 *jalapeño pepper, seeded and minced*
2 *teaspoons minced fresh ginger*
½ *cup diced apple*
¼ *cup diced banana*
¼ *cup diced pitted peeled mango*
¼ *cup golden raisins*
¼ *cup sliced almonds*
 – *pinch of cayenne pepper*
 – *cilantro chiffonade, for garnish*

Rinse and drain the basmati rice. Place the rice in a small saucepan
with 2½ cups of water and a pinch of salt. Bring the rice to a boil over
high heat, then lower the heat to medium and simmer for 10 minutes,
or until most of the water has been absorbed. Place a tight fitting lid on
the pan, then remove the pan from the heat and let sit for another 10
minutes or until all the water is absorbed and the rice is tender. Spread
the rice out on a sheet pan and chill.

Heat the olive oil in a large nonstick sauté pan over high heat. Add the
scallions, jalapeño and ginger and very quickly toss until fragrant. Add
2½ cups of the chilled cooked rice, apple, banana, mango, raisins and
almonds and season to taste with salt, pepper and cayenne.

Transfer the fried rice to a platter. Garnish with cilantro and serve hot.

PIÑA COLADA

Perhaps the most famous tropical drink, the piña colada is a refreshing cocktail made with a simple mixture of pineapple, coconut milk and light rum.

MAKES 4 COCKTAILS

1   *cup light rum*
1   *cup pineapple juice*
1   *cup unsweetened coconut milk*
½   *cup fresh pineapple chunks*
1½ *cups ice cubes*
4   *fresh pineapple slices, for garnish*

Combine the rum, pineapple chunks, coconut milk and pineapple juice in a blender and blend well. Add the ice and blend until slushy.

Pour the piña colada into 4 tall glasses. Garnish each glass with a pineapple slice and serve.

TROPICAL SALAD

Hearts of palm are the edible interior portion of the stem of a cabbage palm tree. Their flavor and texture are similar to an artichoke. Tossed with fresh field greens, mango, tomato and avocado, this salad is a beautiful mix of color and fresh, tropical flavor.

SERVES 4

2   *tablespoons fresh lemon juice*
2   *tablespoons fresh lime juice*
1   *teaspoon grated fresh ginger*
½   *teaspoon grated lime zest*
–   *fine sea salt and freshly ground black pepper*
6   *tablespoons canola oil*
6   *ounces baby field greens*
1   *mango, peeled, pitted, and diced*
1   *avocado, halved, pitted, peeled, and diced*
1   *medium tomato, cored, halved, and cut into ¼-inch-thick slices*
4   *ounces hearts of palm, cut into ¼-inch-thick slices (optional)*
½   *cup fresh mint leaves, torn*

Whisk the lemon juice, lime juice, ginger and zest in a bowl to blend. Season to taste with salt and pepper. Slowly drizzle in the canola oil, while whisking constantly, until well blended. Set aside.

Place the greens, mango, avocado, tomato, hearts of palm and mint in a large bowl and season with salt and pepper. Lightly dress the salad with the vinaigrette and gently toss to combine. Divide the salad equally on 4 chilled plates. Serve immediately.

CAYMANIAN CEVICHE

This is essentially a classic ceviche with a strange, British-influenced, Caymanian twist. HP Sauce is a commercially bottled sauce from England. It has a malt vinegar base mixed with fruit and spices. Because the Cayman Islands are a British territory, Caymanians were exposed to this product and now use it in many recipes and as a condiment.

SERVES 4

- 12 *ounces sushi-grade fish fillet,*
  such as red snapper or tuna
- – *fine sea salt and freshly ground white pepper*
- ¼ *cup thinly sliced red onion*
- 1 *small tomato, peeled, seeded, and diced*
- 2 *tablespoons HP Sauce (see note)*
- 1 *teaspoon Tabasco*
- 3 *limes*
- – *water crackers*

Thinly slice the fish fillet and place the sliced fish in a large bowl. Generously season the fish with salt and pepper. Add the onion, tomato, HP Sauce and Tabasco, then toss lightly to coat. Squeeze the limes over the ceviche and toss lightly again.

Divide the ceviche evenly into small bowls and serve with water crackers.

Note: HP Sauce is a popular brand of brown sauce from the United Kingdom, used extensively in the Cayman Islands. If unavailable at your local market, substitute A1 or another good steak sauce.

SEARED SHRIMP, BABY SPINACH, MÂCHE AND MUSHROOMS WITH WHITE BALSAMIC VINAIGRETTE —*adapted from Le Bernardin*

The flavor of white balsamic vinegar, which is milder than its darker cousin, enhances rather than covers up this fresh salad of greens and seared shrimp. The mushrooms add an earthy quality that balances the dish.

SERVES 4

WHITE BALSAMIC VINAIGRETTE

- 4 *tablespoons butter*
- 2 *tablespoons sherry vinegar*
- 2 *tablespoons white balsamic vinegar*
- – *fine sea salt and freshly ground*
  black pepper
- 3 *tablespoons extra virgin olive oil*

SALAD

- 2 *tablespoons canola oil, divided*
- 6 *ounces fresh hen of the woods mushrooms*
  (maitake), trimmed
- – *fine sea salt and freshly ground white pepper*
- 12 *large shrimp, peeled and deveined*
- 4 *ounces baby spinach leaves*
- 2 *ounce petite mâche*

Cook the butter in a small pan over medium-high heat, whisking occasionally, until golden brown. Pour the brown butter into a bowl and whisk in the sherry vinegar and balsamic vinegar. Season with salt and pepper. Add the olive oil in a steady stream, whisking constantly, until fully emulsified.

Heat 1 tablespoon of the canola oil in a sauté pan over medium-high heat. Add the mushrooms and season with salt and pepper. Cook the mushrooms until golden brown, about 5 minutes. Set aside.

Heat the remaining 1 tablespoon of canola oil in a nonstick sauté pan over medium-high heat. Season the shrimp with salt and pepper and cook the shrimp for 1 to 2 minutes on each side. Transfer the shrimp to a baking sheet lined with paper towels.

Place a pile of spinach leaves in the center of 4 plates, place 3 to 4 mushrooms on top of each pile of spinach, and shingle 3 shrimp on top of each salad. Top each with a few leaves of mâche. Drizzle the vinaigrette over and around the salad and serve immediately.

277

GRILLED PORK CHOPS WITH JERK SPICES

Jerk seasoning, a traditional blend of Caribbean spices including allspice, ginger, cinnamon, nutmeg and cayenne, is rubbed onto the pork chops and allowed to soak into the meat. The seasoning is strong, but as it cooks, the fat from the meat mellows the spices a bit.

SERVES 4

- 2 *shallots, sliced*
- 3 *garlic cloves, sliced*
- 1-2 *Scotch bonnet peppers or habañero peppers (to taste), seeded and sliced*
- 2 *teaspoons thyme leaves*
- – *coarse sea salt or kosher salt*
- ¾ *cup olive oil*
- 3 *tablespoons brown sugar*
- 1 *tablespoon cracked black pepper*
- 2 *teaspoons ground allspice*
- 2 *teaspoons ground cinnamon*
- 2 *teaspoons ground ginger*
- ½ *teaspoon ground nutmeg*
- ¼ *teaspoon cayenne pepper*
- 4 *(8- to 10-ounce) pork chops*
- 1 *lime, cut into 4 wedges*

Place the shallots, garlic, Scotch bonnet pepper and thyme leaves in a mortar and add a pinch of coarse salt. Gently mash with the pestle and stir in the olive oil. Transfer the chili-garlic oil to a small container and set aside.

Stir together the brown sugar, cracked pepper, allspice, cinnamon, ginger, nutmeg and cayenne in a small bowl. Generously season the pork chops with the spice mixture and spoon a tablespoon of the chili-garlic oil over the pork chops. Cover and refrigerate for at least 1 hour and up to 3 hours.

When ready to cook, remove the chops from the refrigerator and let them come to room temperature. Prepare the charcoal grill, letting the coals burn down to medium heat, 15 to 20 minutes.

Season the pork chops with coarse salt and grill the chops for 7 to 10 minutes on each side, depending on thickness, or until cooked through and a meat thermometer registers 150°F. As the pork chops grill, move them around, as necessary, to manage the heat of the grill. Transfer the chops to a platter and let rest for at least 5 minutes.

Serve the pork chops with more of the chili-garlic oil and lime wedges.

MAHI MAHI WITH GRILLED MANGO
AND ROASTED CHILI SAUCE   SERVES 4

Grilling pieces of mango over burning charcoal intensifies the mango's flavor and
caramelizes its natural sugars. The sweet fruit blends very nicely with hot spices
and mahi mahi, which is a perfect fish for grilling.

1	*large red bell pepper*
1	*teaspoon canola oil plus*
	more for brushing
1	*shallot, thinly sliced*
1	*garlic clove, thinly sliced*
2	*dried ancho peppers, seeds*
	removed and rehydrated
–	*fine sea salt and freshly ground*
	white pepper
4	*tablespoons unsalted butter*
4	*mangoes, peeled, pitted,*
	and quartered
2	*tablespoons olive oil*
¼	*cup fresh lime juice*
¼	*cup cilantro leaves, julienned*
4	*(6-ounce) mahi mahi fillets*

Place the whole red bell pepper on a gas burner or in a broiler and roast until
the skin is black and blistered. Transfer the roasted pepper to a paper bag or
a resealable plastic bag, then seal the bag and let the pepper steam for 5 minutes. Remove the pepper from the bag, rub off the skin and remove the seeds.

Heat 1 tablespoon of the canola oil in a medium saucepan over medium-
high heat. Add the shallot, garlic and roasted red bell pepper and sauté until
they start to soften, 2 to 3 minutes. Add the rehydrated ancho peppers and
1½ cups of water; simmer for 15 to 20 minutes, or until the flavors come
together. Season to taste with salt and pepper. Transfer the sauce to a blender,
add the butter and blend until smooth. Transfer the sauce to a small saucepan and set aside until ready to use.

Prepare the charcoal grill, letting the charcoals burn down to medium heat,
15 to 20 minutes.

When the barbecue is ready, lightly oil the grill rack with canola oil. Place
the mango quarters in a bowl and season to taste with salt and pepper.
Drizzle the olive oil over the mangoes and carefully place the mango pieces
on the grill. Grill until the mangoes are nicely colored on all sides, about 5
minutes. Transfer the grilled mangoes back to the bowl and toss with the
lime juice and cilantro.

Meanwhile, season the mahi mahi with salt and pepper. Grill the fish for
about 3 minutes on each side, or until it is just warm in the center; a metal
skewer should be easily inserted into the fish and, when left in for 5 seconds,
feel just warm when touched to the lip.

Plate 4 pieces of the grilled mangoes in the center of each of 4 plates.
Bring the sauce to a boil and adjust the seasoning. Place the grilled mahi
mahi on top of the mangoes. Spoon the sauce over and around the fish
and serve immediately.

COCONUT RICE PUDDING   SERVES 4

This is just like a classic rice pudding but includes ginger, lemongrass and lime juice
to help cut through the sweetness a bit.

¾   *cup unsweetened coconut milk*
¾   *cup whole milk*
¼   *cup water*
1   *stalk lemongrass, thinly sliced*
1   *tablespoon chopped fresh ginger*
½   *vanilla bean, split lengthwise*
¾   *cup short-grain rice*
1   *ripe mango, peeled, pitted, and finely diced*
¼   *cup plus 2 tablespoons granulated sugar*
2   *tablespoons finely chopped candied ginger*
1   *lime, juiced*

Combine the coconut milk, milk, water, lemongrass and fresh
ginger in a heavy saucepan. Scrape the seeds from the vanilla bean
into the coconut milk mixture, then add the bean. Bring to a boil,
then remove from the heat. Cover and infuse for 15 minutes.

Meanwhile, blanch the rice by placing it in a separate saucepan
with enough cold water to cover. Bring just to a boil, then strain
and reserve.

Strain the coconut milk infusion through a fine-mesh sieve.
Combine the infused coconut milk with the rice in a saucepan and
gently bring to a boil. Reduce the heat to low, cover, and cook for
30 to 40 minutes, or until the rice is tender. Remove from the heat
and cool slightly.

Stir in the mango, sugar, candied ginger and lime juice. Serve
warm or chilled.

THANKS

Avec Eric is the fruit of a great collaboration between very inspired, creative and talented individuals. It has been a fun learning adventure where very often we actually learned the hard way, probably because of our pure naïve vision and intention—exactly like a 5-year old child would discover the world and it is priceless and magical and totally worth it.

I am excited, humbled and endlessly grateful to share the fruit of our labor with my long and complex family made up of the Riperts, Le Bernardin, the Anomaly gang and, of course, the entire team and crew behind *Avec Eric*.

Justin, Geoff and Soa, you have been the driving and creative force to materialize our dream. However, there is a very long list of much beloved members of the "family" that I would like to thank equally for their unwavering support—Mum, Sandra, Adrien, the other members of my family from the Talon side—Maguy, Mandy, Chris and Coco.

Thank you to Angie for capturing the spirit of *Avec Eric* in your beautiful photos and words. Thank you Adrienne for your hard work and Kim for your encouragement and guidance.

Thank you so much to those of you who opened your doors to us and helped us along the way—David Kinch, Dan Barber, José Andrés, David Chang, Grant Achatz, Dean Fearing, Gail Simmons, Keiko Nicollini and Michael Ryan—and everyone else we met on the journey. Tony, thank you so much for your participation and friendship.

Special thanks to Michael, Aldo, Ben, David and to everyone else at Le Bernardin, who support me every day.

ACKNOWLEDGEMENTS

SPONSORS AND PARTNERS

Acqua Panna / American Public Television / Anomaly / Billy Reid /
Blanco / CaesarStone / Cayman Airways / Cayman Board of Tourism /
Cuisinart / KQED / Lenox / Michael Ryan and the Dragon Bay Resort / Miele /
Olympus / PoggenPohl / Ritz-Carlton Grand Cayman / Steven Alan /
Tag Worldwide, USA / Wine.com / Whole Foods Market

ANOMALY

Justin Barocas / Heather Brown / Mike Byrne / Jim Conlon /
Jason Deland / Carl Johnson / Josh Line / Andrew Loevenguth / Kevin Lyons /
Michelle Morales / Angie Mosier / Richard Mulder / Nikelle Orellana /
Gino Reyes / Hank Romero / Beam Seiladom / Jennifer Smith /
Jordan Spielman / Johnny Vulkan / Jon Zast

AVEC ERIC TELEVISION SHOW

Dominick Ciardiello / Geoffrey Drummond / Karen Giberson / Alan Hereford /
Dean Miller / Fred Siegel / Paul Swensen / Tomas Tucker

LE BERNARDIN

Adrienne Cheatham / Soa Davies / Eric Gestel / Michael Laiskonis /
Maguy Le Coze / Chris Muller / Mandy Oser / Cathy Sheary / Aldo Sohm

CHEFS

Grant Achatz / José Andrés / Dan Barber / Anthony Bourdain /
David Chang / Dean Fearing / David Kinch / Gail Simmons

PUBLISHING PARTNERS

Pamela Chirls / Diana Cisek / Julie Schilder / Kim Witherspoon

284

ERIC RIPERT RESTAURANTS

LE BERNARDIN
155 West 51st Street, New York City
le-bernardin.com

10 ARTS by ERIC RIPERT
10 Avenue of the Arts, Philadelphia
10arts.com

BLUE by ERIC RIPERT
The Ritz-Carlton, Grand Cayman

WESTEND BISTRO
1190 22nd Street NW, Washington DC
westendbistrodc.com

ALSO BY ERIC RIPERT

**LE BERNARDIN COOKBOOK:
FOUR-STAR SIMPLICITY**
by Eric Ripert and Maguy LeCoze

A RETURN TO COOKING
by Eric Ripert and Michael Ruhlman

ON THE LINE
by Eric Ripert and Christine Muhlke

INDEX

287

293

AVEC ERIC